THE UNTOLD SECRET OF HER BEAUTY

THE UNTOLD SECRET OF HER BEAUTY

A STORY OF DESPERATION TO INSPIRATION

JUPSHY JASMIN

Untold Secret Beauty, LLC

Contents

Acknowledgment	1
Introduction	**3**
1 Desperation	6
2 Devotion	11
3 The Praise of Leah Echoes	25
4 Leah Became the Bloodline of Jesus	30
5 How Jesus Dealt with Rejection	39
6 Leah's Honorable Burial	44
7 Self-Image	49
8 The Perception of Beauty is Subjective	52
9 I am Beautiful	61
10 Love Yourself- Redeem Your God-Given Power	69
Appendix	83
References	93
Untold Secret Beauty Publisher	95

Acknowledgment

Dr. Eva Francis, thank you for responding to God's calling. This has been a great experience for me.

Ruth Anoice, I appreciate your friendship. I love your energy. Thank you for collaborating with me. May God continue to open doors of opportunities for you.

Roosevelt Jean, thank you for being so responsive to my request. You are an amazing photographer. May God continue to bless your creativity.

Judine Jasmin, I am lost for words. You are not only a sister but a dependable friend. You are always ready to assist me in every way possible. I thank God for you.

Juliam Jasmin, no matter how crazy my ideas may sound, you always give me your undivided attention. I hope that God rebirths your inner creativity. The world has been patiently waiting to hear your message. This is a call to action. Come on board!

Thank you to all my friends and family for your support and encouragement!

Introduction

"Every time I thought I was being rejected from something good, I was actually being re-directed to something better."
— Steve Maraboli

Leah's story from the book of Genesis in the Holy Bible has always had a special place in my heart. In the Bible, Leah was the first daughter of Laban, Rachel's older sister, Jacob's first wife, and the mother to seven of Jacob's children. She is best known as the ugly sister who endured years of emotional hardship.

For many years, I've believed that Leah's story was one of defeat; all she wanted was to experience love from her husband, and though she prayed faithfully, God repeatedly ignored her desperate cry. In the end, it seems that she died without her prayer answered.

However, a profound truth dawned on me one day. We all encounter moments of rejection and resistance in our lives, whether in relationships, careers, or self-esteem. But in contrast to dwelling in fear, we can embrace rejections and objections as opportunities to move forward.

In the face of obstacles, it's oh-so tempting to give up and give in. But guess what? It's not the only thing that will help you conquer objections and rejection. The key to strength and resilience is to embrace these times of rejection. Difficulties are an essential part of learning and growth.

Jacob may not have loved Leah, but God undoubtedly did. Leah exemplifies faith through God's silence and teaches us to trust God, even when we cannot trace Him; God's silence does not indicate that He is inactive. This revelation changed my life.

God is always at work, even when we can't see it. This understanding gave me the courage to face the unknown and to take comfort in knowing that God is always in control, providing me with peace and assurance that everything would be alright.

God revealed to me that Leah's story is not just a depressing, ancient biblical story of two sisters involved in a love triangle. Leah's story, legacy, and contribution to the Jewish and Christian faiths have made remarkable history. Her linage continues to bless us today. Although Leah's experience was painful, she was a great woman of faith whose empowering message reminds us that our trust in God will not go unnoticed. It's a story of hope and resilience. It shows that even in the darkest times, there is still hope to be found.

According to Hebrews 13:5, the confidence we have as children of God is that He will never leave us helpless or without support. God's plan for his children's lives is to prosper us and give us hope and a future (Jeremiah 29:11, NIV). Even when situations place us at a disadvantage, or others may overlook us, we do not need others' approval to live a fruitful and abundant life.

God's rating scale is unbiased and nondiscriminatory. Do not be discouraged because God sees you exactly where you are. While others will judge you by your appearance, where you are from, and what you did, God's scale surpasses these conditional earthly criteria. He is our source of strength and provision and will never leave us.

Leah's story proves that societal inequalities related to physical imperfections have existed since ancient history. Yet despite her challenges, Leah succeeded by embracing her unique beauty and strength. Leah's story also serves as a reminder that it's okay to be different and to celebrate our differences. We should never strive to be like everyone else and instead strive to be the best version of ourselves by embracing our uniqueness and using it to our advantage. She has shown us that anything is possible with a positive attitude and a bit of courage.

I am not writing this book to paraphrase the story of Leah; it is too empowering to duplicate. This book provides a new perspective and empowerment towards social standards and self-love. I want women to read this book to gain confidence about themselves through Leah's story and inspire them to realize they can succeed no matter their obstacles.

I truly believe that Leah's journey to magnificent glory is the testimony many of us have longed for. We should all strive to be more like her: to celebrate what makes us special and to become genuinely remarkable without outside validation. You, and you alone, define what success means for yourself. We should focus on our own goals, values, and beliefs and use them to create our unique path to success.

It is time to end comparing attractiveness and the obsession with beauty enhancement and embark on the journey of confidence in God, accepting the body He has blessed you with. You are beautiful in God's eyes because He created you in His image!

Let's dig deep and discover your untold secret beauty!

1

Desperation

Leah had weak eyes, but Rachel had a lovely figure and was beautiful.
Genesis 29:17

Take a moment to think about your own life. Have you ever been compared to another woman? How did that make you feel?

Jacob, the son of Isaac and Rebekah, was instructed to find a wife from his mother's side. Jacob ran to the city of Haran in Northwest Mesopotamia to meet with his uncle, Rebekah's brother, Laban. Upon his arrival, he met Rachel at the well and instantly fell in love with her.

As her father, Laban, welcomed him, he struck a deal with Jacob: Jacob would work seven years for Laban, and in turn, Laban would give him Rachel's hand in marriage. Due to the family ties, Jacob trusted Laban through a verbal agreement without questioning the land's marriage customs. Jacob worked his heart out in exchange for what he thought would be Rachel.

However, Laban exploited Jacob's ignorance. Since Leah was the oldest daughter, she should be married first. However, Rachel was much more beautiful than Leah, and Laban had no faith she would be married unless he stepped in. To comply with this custom, Laban concocted a deceitful plan.

Let's try to imagine the day of their wedding. Knowing that he had completed his agreed labor, Jacob could not wait to finally have the wife he had worked towards all these years. Laban arranged a big feast and brought out his daughter, who wore a heavy veil. Given the occasion, Jacob was likely inebriated and did not realize that Leah was under the veil instead of Rachel.

Imagine Leah getting ready for her big day, filled with excitement. The preparations, the festivity, and the people came out to witness the marital celebration. Stirred with bridal jitters, Leah tried on her veil one last time. In Leah's culture, being married was an honor, and Leah must have been waiting for this moment her whole life. Her dream was coming true. Being married and bearing children would give her a sense of purpose.

At the end of the night, Leah was the happiest she had ever been as she rested in her husband's arms.

The next morning, Jacob's sudden jump out of bed woke Leah from her blissful slumber. She arose to find the look of pure shock and horror on Jacob's face. He seemed confused, and his whole body was shaking. Before Leah could say a word, Jacob ran out of the room angrily. Leah did not understand what was going on with her husband. That was not the reaction she expected the morning after their wedding celebration. Leah could not help but get up and follow her husband. But before she could catch up to him, her heart dropped. She heard shouting between Jacob and Laban outside.

Her father had tricked Jacob into marrying her, and Jacob was willing to be in servitude for an additional seven years for her beautiful sister, Rachel.

Leah was crushed. She tried to remain strong, but her strength failed her. Leah fell to the floor with tears running down her face.

Have you ever been rejected before?

By the end of the first week of marriage to Leah, Jacob took his second wife. Jacob accepted working for a total of fourteen years just for Rachel. However, the Bible never explained why Jacob loved Rachel other than her physical attractiveness, so his love seems purely physical.

Due to her lack of conventional beauty, Leah was denied the experience of being loved by Jacob, leaving her to doubt her self-worth. This rejection brought her to a state of insecurity and gave her a desperate need for validation. Unfortunately, those viewed as unattractive by societal standards are overlooked and miss out on life's opportunities.

Like Laban felt the need to hide Leah under a veil, society will hide you to impersonate someone you are not. This is a tactic used by influencers because of their opinion of beauty and lack of perception.

How would you feel in Leah's situation?

Leah's story may not appear to have any significance or relevance to our contemporary Western culture. Why should it? After all, it took place many centuries before the birth of Christ. However, Leah's experience, pain, and setbacks are no different than the harsh reality many people face today.

If you've ever been overlooked or judged by society because you did not meet their standards of attractiveness, you can relate to Leah. She was a victim of physical attractiveness discrimination, also known as lookism. Discrimination isolates individuals from society, decreases their life satisfaction, and increases their loneliness. However, Leah's encounter with physical attractiveness discrimination also teaches us how revealing our inner attractiveness and engaging in healthy behaviors will change the course of one's story.

Allow me to fast-forward to the 21st century and show you how relatable Leah's experience is.

It only takes a second to form an impression of someone, whether it's face-to-face, online, or in a photo. The physical appearance of others predominantly influences our image of their personality traits, desirability, and opportunities. This stereotype creates an attractiveness bias when we associate goodness with beauty and horror with the opposite. For example, the perception of facial appearance is often correlated with health by providing information on signs of disease.

Contrary to popular belief, facial attractiveness is not an accurate indicator of health status. It is often a misleading predictor that can mistakenly rank actual sick people as healthy if their beauty suppresses the genuine recognition of their health (Talamas, Mavor, and Perrett, 2016). Due to medical advancement, there is a significant increase in survival rate and life quality, and it is difficult to identify a healthy versus unhealthy person purely based on physical appearance.

Regarding mental illness, physically attractive individuals receive higher positive perceptions toward social and personality traits, supporting the attractiveness stereotype. In the clinical setting, the more attractive a patient is, the more positive ratings and care they receive (Garstkiewicz, 2014). Many conventionally attractive individuals with mental illness go undiagnosed by society due to their charm and good looks.

Even though physical attractiveness has proven to be an unreliable indicator of health, society places so much emphasis on physical appearance. Hollywood's super glamorous beauty perfection often leads us to appearance comparison; we evaluate our self-worth based on social media portrayals and sociocultural preferences, resulting in internalizing negative thoughts. At this point, we accept these ideal preferences and engage in unhealthy behaviors to meet the standards.

This is just one example of beauty being skin-deep, subjective, and nothing more. The approval of society based on your outer beauty is not the only and ultimate factor of your fate or destiny. Leah had to learn this lesson before her strength could be renewed.

To Be Unloved

When the Lord saw that Leah was not loved, he enabled her to conceive, but Rachel remained childless.
Genesis 29:31

Leah was not giving up without a fight. She picked up all the pieces of her broken heart and went on a quest to win Jacob's heart. However, Jacob did not love Leah. He resented her. After all, Jacob was tricked into marrying her and never considered Leah his wife. Jacob didn't even wait to find out if she was barren or fertile.

Leah was treated more like a concubine or servant while Jacob spent most of his nights with Rachel. The more Jacob neglected her, the more she longed for his love. Her obsession built until Jacob became an idol to her.

Leah had desperately devoted all her confidence to someone she thought would give her a sense of being loved. She believed that if she could give Jacob what he wanted, she could win his heart, and her life would have the meaning she fantasized about.

Doesn't that sound familiar, laboring for approval and validation from others?

2

Devotion

Life is based on the decision that we make. When faced with unpleasant circumstances, it is easy to revert to the negative and start complaining. Instead, Leah took on a different approach, which takes a lot of strength. Leah prayed. Through the power of her prayers, she changed her destiny and impacted an entire nation.

Expect provision!

Expect your cup to overflow because God blesses us with abundance in times of difficulty. His blessings are not limited to the material but include spiritual benefits according to His perfect will and timing. As seen with Leah, He may not always grant our petition, but His blessings are still in our best interest.

Often, we don't realize the power of our prayers. If we did, we would be on our knees more, crying out for God's intervention. Miracles happen because there is power in prayer, after all. Prayer opens our eyes and sheds light on our dark moments in life. When you devote yourself to prayer and thanksgiving unto God, He will intervene in his glorious and sovereign, majestic power. It is an experience that is everlasting. He hears the cry of the humble hearts; Leah can attest to that.

We may not know how to pray initially, but as we start to pray, the spirit of God begins to anchor our hearts to align with His will. It's like working out your muscles. The more repetitions, the more assertive you become. We become stronger and more resistant to the day-to-day struggles in front of us.

In this chapter, we witness Leah's spiritual journey. Jacob's attitude didn't change during this journey, nor did he acknowledge her as his first wife. But we can see the strength and growth in her time of relentless agony, how wisdom shone through her as she prayed. Prayer gives us hope and opens new doors, magnifying our lives with His riches. No one who prays to God is ever disappointed.

Reuben: Behold a Son

Leah became pregnant and gave birth to a son. She named him **Reuben**, *for she said, "It is because the Lord has seen my misery. Surely my husband will love me now."*

Genesis 29:32

God blessed Leah's womb at a time when she was emotionally vulnerable. Leah knew that although Jacob did not love her, she would find favor in his eyes by giving him a son—after all, the woman Jacob was madly in love with was barren. Leah named her firstborn son Reuben, meaning "behold a son."

Like Leah, don't you know that God has seen your misery? Perhaps you're in a situation and feel that you're all alone. But God sees you and wants to give you a Reuben to comfort you during the painful periods of your life.

To learn more about the life of Reuben, turn to Appendix A.

Simeon: To Hear

She conceived again, and when she gave birth to a son, she said, "Because the LORD heard that I am not loved, he gave me this one too." So, she named him **Simeon**.

Genesis 29:33

Leah's childbirth benediction continued. She gave birth to a second son and named him Simeon, meaning "to hear." Leah believed that God gave her this second son because her prayers reached from her lips to His ears. However, even after Leah gave him a second son, Jacob's attitude toward her did not change.

How many of you are in a situation that needs to be heard by God?

To learn more about the life of Simeon, turn to Appendix A.

Levi: Joined

Again, she conceived, and when she gave birth to a son, she said, "Now, at last, my husband will become attached to me because I have borne him three sons." So, he was named **Levi**.

Genesis 29:34

I am pretty sure that you would agree that insanity is doing the same thing over and over while expecting a different result. Well, Leah continued praying for Jacob's love, and his attitude did not change after Leah conceived their first or second son. She thought three would make a difference and fantasized that Jacob would cling to her because of their sons.

In these cultures, fertility was highly regarded and closely associated with a woman's femininity. Some religions worshiped fertility, sex, and childbirth because they brought life and prosperity. The greatest gift a wife could give her husband was a son, as men have historically favored boys as their firstborn.

By now, Jacob saw that Leah had given him sons, and God heard her prayers and let them unite. Leah was desperately seeking not only attention but a committed relationship. She wanted the two to become one, just like the Bible designed a wife and husband to be. Leah longed to be attached to Jacob.

Leah's compulsive behavior was a cry for help. The agony that Leah was experiencing was excruciating because social rejection causes pain. The "pain" she experienced as she watched Jacob spend countless nights with Rachel was more than a figure of speech. She was his first wife, so Jacob should have been with her.

To learn more about the life of Levi, turn to Appendix A.

Rejection is Painful

Scientists have used MRIs to demonstrate how recalling social rejection triggers the same neurons as a physical pain experience. This "social pain" can be defined as social injury from the perception of actual or potential psychological threats or detachment from close others or social groups (Eisenberger and Lieberman, 2004). Both types of pain are distressing and share a general resemblance in the somatosensory brain system.

When we are born, we are relatively immature and unable to care for ourselves. We strongly depend on close caregivers during our infancy for nourishment and protection. As we get older and more independent, our ties to social groups remain critical to our survival in other ways. Now, we benefit from the shared responsibility of a collective society, thus creating the body of Christ, where many members have different functions belonging to one Lord (Romans 12:3-5; 1 Corinthians 12:12).

In this way, social rejection harms our survival on many spectrums. It may seem unfair to have this physical-social pain overlap because the feelings that follow a broken relationship or a failed marriage are undoubtedly painful. It will put you in a vulnerable state for an extended period. God designed us to avoid social disconnections and maintain social closeness through the pain signals triggered during social separation. Conversely, connecting with others is likely to increase one's chances of staying alive and reproducing (Chester, DeWall & Pond, 2016).

The emotional pain that Leah endured was equivalent to the physical pain of someone pouring a cup of hot steaming coffee on her arm, which is why Leah's pain was not taken lightly by God.

How Leah's Seed Was Joined with God

Leah never asked for royal recognition or religious authority in her prayer. She had no idea that God was stirring up a blessing amid her agony and opening the flood gates of Heaven that would cause her cup to run over.

God saw that Jacob did not love Leah, so God blessed Leah's womb (Deuteronomy 7:13). The tribe of her third son, Levi, became priests. Priests had special religious responsibilities regarding the Israelites and were joined with God. This was the only tribe designated to represent the people before God and offer sacrifice by the law. As a result, the other tribes were expected to provide tithes to the priests working in the Temple of Jerusalem. They could not possess lands because God was their inheritance (Joshua 13:33).

The following section explains the historical and religious significance of biblical figures such as Moses and John the Baptist. In Appendix B, the historical and religious importance of additional biblical figures from Levi's tribe, such as Eleazar, Eli, Ezra, Samuel, Malachi, and Aaron, are detailed. We must identify who they were and highlight their contribution to the faith to understand how Leah's seed was joined with God and why the Levite tribe was essential and powerful.

Moses: Let My People Go!

Leah is the great-great-grandmother of Moses and Aaron. Both parents of the brothers were Levites. Although Jacob's favorite son, Joseph, the son of Rachel, rescued the family from famine, Moses took Israel's nation out of Egypt. He also parted the Red Sea for the Israelites to flee on dry feet from the enslavement of the pharaoh and enter the Promised Land.

The Levites, once scattered because of the sin of incest, were given another chance—God turned their curse into a blessing. The tribe became the leading Israelite tribe in the time of Moses, where Moses would also bless his tribe by atoning for their founder's sin. A tribe that was once scattered was now the priests of the whole Israelite nation.

The Levites became a sacrifice of thanksgiving for God's deliverance from the bondage in Egypt, and He consecrated them to his service.

Since the Levites were initially excluded from the land distribution, they were best suited to service, requiring them to live throughout Canaan. If they did possess land like the other Tribes of Israel, they would have been limited in the scope of their responsibilities. They were assigned to different cities based on the son of Levi (Joshua 21). In the wilderness, they were strategically settled, encircling the tribe of Levi.

The Levites provided the people with instructions, cared for the tabernacle, and led tent meetings. They were the only tribe with authorized access to the territory and responsible for managing all the tabernacle's day-to-day operations. The sons of Aaron had the highest rank as the "anointed priests."

The Levites were an integral tribe of the nation of Israel, shaping its history significantly. Through all the wandering and conquest, their sole responsibility and commitment to the sanctuary kept the nation grounded under the Israelite law.

John the Baptist: Prepared the Way of the Lord

Jesus also said, "Truly I tell you, among those born of women there has not risen anyone greater than John the Baptist, yet whoever is least in the kingdom of heaven is greater than he."

Matthew 11:11

In the New Testament, we are introduced to Zachariah and Elizabeth, both descendants of Aaron from Levi's tribe. They were a childless elderly couple. One day, as Zachariah was in the temple burning incense, the angel Gabriel appeared to the Leviticus priest. This was the first spiritual encounter since the 400 years of silence after Malachi's judgment in the Old Testament.

In the New Testament's opening, the children of Israel had lost their royal dominance to the descendant of Esau, Herod the Great. The Aaronic priests were still worshiping and conducting the roles and responsibilities Moses's law had ordered, but they were limited only to the Jewish temple.

Gabriel broke the 400 years of silence, and Zachariah's prayers were finally answered (Luke 1:13-17). He would not bear a son like any average couple. Instead, God chose them to bear a son that would be the forerunner of the prophesied Messiah. His name would be "John." While in the womb, he would be filled with the Holy Spirit and be set apart for the Lord's service.

That prophecy came to pass when Jesus's mother, Mary, visited her cousin, Elizabeth. At the time, both women were pregnant. John leaped for joy in his mother's womb at the sound of Mary's voice, and Elizabeth was filled with the Holy Spirit (Luke 1:39-41). Due to both parents' Aaronic lineage, John's priesthood authority was legitimate and would forever go down as the greatest prophet ever to serve the Kingdom of God. His ministry was prophesied in the Old Testament by Isaiah and Malachi (Isaiah 40:3; Malachi 3:1).

In the Old Testament, all the kings of Israel and their successors were anointed by Levites. For instance, Samuel anointed King Saul and King David. However, this time, John the Baptist transferred the Old Covenant God had with the Levites to a New Covenant through Jesus Christ.

John the Baptist's life was entirely devoted and surrendered to the coming of the Messiah. He was entrusted with the unique task of baptizing the people to forgive sin. He preached repentance and the gospel, turning many unto the Lord. But he never imagined that he would have the honor of baptizing the Messiah himself because Jesus was sinless and did not need baptism. It was a unique, once-in-a-lifetime experience that only John the Baptist shared with Christ.

Leah prayed to be joined with Jacob. God created a divine covenant with Leah and her linage through the tribe of Levi. The heavens opened that day in the Jordan River, and the Holy Spirit descended like a dove. Leah's prayer had come to pass. Through her son Levi, she was joined through an eternal alliance with a God who loved her unconditionally.

Leah prayed for a temporary covenant with Jacob, but the heavens and Earth's Creator gave her a divine covenant that blessed her beyond measure for generations to come. According to Revelation's book, Levi's tribe was listed among the twelve tribes in the New Jerusalem.

But you are a chosen people, a royal priesthood, a holy nation, God's special possession, that you may declare the praises of him who called you out of darkness into his marvelous light.
1 Peter 2:9

Judah: Praise

She conceived again, and when she gave birth to a son, she said, "This time, I will praise the Lord." So she named him Judah. Then she stopped having children.

Genesis 29:35

The Bible doesn't tell us what happened, but there is a shift in the narrative. Leah conceived again. However, this time, she was not seeking to please her husband. With her fourth child, she said, "Now I will Praise the Lord." She named him "Judah," meaning "praise."

As Charles R. Swindoll said in *The Grace Awakening*, life is 10% what happens to you and 90% how you react to it. Attitude is everything in a situation. We have all endured rejection, failure, loss, and heartache at least once—it's inevitable. But you can decide to look at the cup half-empty or half-full.

Take responsibility for the one thing you can control: your attitude. A negative mindset will submerge you in your sorrows, but a positive attitude will give you a greater perspective on life and elevate you to new heights. You can choose to live the life you want, no matter what curveballs are thrown at you, if your mentality decides to achieve greatness. You must be willing to do the inside job to overcome bad situations. Be strong and not let life defeat you when things go south; remember that every hardship hides opportunity.

Life is short. Do not let bad situations create a roadblock on your path to destiny. Instead, let thanksgiving be embedded in your heart because that's when extraordinary things will begin to happen. Your attitude determines your altitude.

Leah realized that she could not control the way Jacob felt about her. She prayed for God to give him a change of heart, but Jacob remained the same. She could have quickly taken on the victim mentality and asked God, "Why me?" She could have gotten upset at God for not answering her prayers and questioning God's sovereignty. However, Leah was terrific. She remained strong. She decided not to possess a Godly mentality, where all things work together for good for those who love Him (Romans 8:28).

The same goes for you reading this book. Negative feelings from disappointments, rejections, and unmet expectations will always exist because we are emotional beings. How you decide to respond will determine your outcome. In the next section, I want you to think about and understand why your praise is impactful.

Judah's Royal Blessing

Although Judah was the fourth son, he was a man of outstanding leadership. Unlike his older brothers, Judah was consistent in his good deeds, becoming the most appropriate son for birthright and inheritance. Judah was the only son to receive the most prominent, extensive, and prophetic blessings on Jacob's deathbed.

Let's take a moment and dissect what was promised to Judah's linage because I want you to comprehend how praise operates. It creates a domino effect, a ripple effect. Leah praised God when Judah was born, and then Jacob prophesized royal blessings over Judah's descendants on his deathbed.

One single praise shifted a whole generation dramatically!

It impacted history tremendously!

It revolutionized our faith miraculously!

Jacob started his blessing by saying:

"Judah, your brothers will praise you; your hand will be on the neck of your enemies; your father's sons will bow down to you."
Genesis 49:8

Jacob's prophecy over the tribe of Judah foretold their journey and eventual reign. Jacob prophesied that Judah's brothers would praise him. After all, Judah's name means praise. At the time of blessing, Joseph ranked "prince among his brothers" because of his position as Egypt's prime minister. Joseph saved his family from famine, and his dreams of reigning over his family had come to pass. However, Jacob prophesied that his sons would bow down to Judah, not Joseph, as the primary leader.

The bowing of the eleven tribes of Israel to Judah's tribe signified recognition as God's anointed one. Praise was a powerful governing force. It meant that his name would be glorified and boasted, and Judah would be honored by his brothers. The tribe's strength would be in their hands; whether fighting their enemies or playing instruments, they would be praised for working with their hands.

"You are a lion's cub, Judah; you return from the prey, my son. Like a lion, he crouches and lies down, like a lioness—who dares to rouse him?"

Jacob compared Judah to a lion, foretelling the courageous kingship and strength of the leaders, such as King David, would resemble. In this verse, we see the growth and transformation of the Tribe of Judah. First, they start as young lions, describing their immaturity. But as they grew in wisdom, they became mature enough to crouch, stoop, or bend their knees, transitioning to a place of humility, patience, knowledge, and faith. This tranquil spirit would introduce the "Prince of Peace." When they reached their ultimate maturity, their faith would become courageous and unwavering. It would be like none other.

Lions adapted to fight. The tribe of Judah would be preyed on by more powerful nations in their early stages. As they matured with the guidance of God, they would become strong and undefeated through their faith. They would not be as vindictive as a raging lion but warriors in the army of God, enjoying their power and success. They would be watchful in their crouching position and defend their territory and families; a lioness is crucial to the tribe's survival, as they provide prosperity and protection. Their strength could not be matched because they were considered the "king of the jungle," so who could rise against them?

In the wilderness, the encampment of the Israelite tribes was organized precisely by the divine authority of God. The tribe of Judah would always be first in line. Moses was instructed to assign where to place each tribe in relation to the Tent of the Meeting (Numbers 2:3-4). Judah's tribe was given to the outer camp of the east side, the entrance facing the sun's rising, believed to be God's favorite side. Moses and Aaron were encamped inside the tabernacle and placed on the east side. When they broke up to march, the tribe of Judah always took the lead.

"The scepter will not depart from Judah, nor the ruler's staff/rod from between his feet, until he to whom it belongs shall come and the obedience of the nations shall be his."

Jacob blessed Judah with supreme authority. We see that the blessing of the seed of Abraham flowed unto Judah and his descendants, who would go on to become kings. Kings wielded the scepter to signify authority and power over a nation, and the royal benediction that Jacob assigned to Judah would be a unique and royal kingdom.

It appeared that the prophecy had failed at times, for example, during the Babylon exile, when Nebuchadnezzar invaded Judah and besieged the city of Jerusalem. However, the Tribe of Judah would hold the royal power until the Messiah established His kingdom on Earth.

"He will tether his donkey to a vine, his colt to the choicest branch; he will wash his garments in wine, his robes in the blood of grapes."

The previous verse shows that Judah was blessed with a lion-like nature. Then God takes that authority. He asked that it become tamed to receive the anointing of God. He is demanding a sacrifice to make a covenant with his people. This foretold how humanity would establish the Messiah's kingdom on Earth.

The donkey symbolizes wealth, peace, and well-being. They are intuitive animals and personify Christ-like behaviors due to their mild heart, persistence, and adaptability. Additionally, they provide service to others and are resilient and steadfast in their hard work. Jesus would later come riding on a donkey.

Wine represented transformation because grapes had to undergo fermentation before they became wine. The Holy Spirit would wash their garment, cleansing them of carnal and mortal iniquity. This would be done with wine, meaning transformation through His blood.

The blood of grapes represented the abundance of blessing from God and His covenant with the Israelites. God was the True Vine that purifies and fills us with His redeeming grace. It was socially familiar for the ancients to drink wine, and was an essential part of worship. It was used in commemorating the Passover and the Lord's Supper. It was also used as medicine to help the sick (1 Timothy 5:23).

It also prophesied the children of Israel settling in the Promised Land, a land of prosperity. God blessed them with strength, but they were to bring it under the Most-High authority with that strength. As leaders who were set apart, they needed to humble themselves for the cleansing of God. The "choicest branch" represented that His people would be peculiar.

The tribe was the first stone of the high priest's breastplate (Exodus 39:10). Depending on the Bible translation, it would be a precious stone of fiery, red-colored mineral known as sardius, carnelian, or ruby. It represented the Scepter of God and His purified people.

"His eyes will be darker than wine, his teeth whiter than milk."

Usually, when angry, the person's red blood vessels dilate, giving them darker eyes. However, Jacob is not referring to any moody behavior. He refers to a supernatural transformation once the tribe's garment is washed and purified. They would be filled with His blood, bringing them profound insight and wisdom from the Lord.

White represents purity; milk is the primary calcium source, producing strong bones and healthy teeth. Milk also contains fat, which provides energy to the body and represents abundance.

Lionesses are adapted for hunting. They stalk their prey till they reach proximity. Then, they tackle their prey by the throat with their claws or teeth to suffocate them. They have one of the strongest bites in the animal kingdom. Jacob said they would use their hands to attack their enemies, but now we see that they also use their teeth to devour their prey.

Then, one of the elders said to me, "Do not weep! See, the Lion of the tribe of Judah, the Root of David, has triumphed. He can open the scroll and its seven seals."

Then I saw a Lamb, looking as if it had been slain, standing in the center of the throne, encircled by the four living creatures and the elders. He had seven horns and seven eyes: the seven spirits of God sent out into all the Earth.
Revelation 5: 5-6

While the Bible does not explain why Leah praised God with her fourth son, the tribe of Judah would be a blessing that would keep on giving.

Remember, words are powerful. What you say during your most challenging moment when your back is up against a wall and there seems to be no hope can either make you or break you. It is the most critical time to avoid the temptation of feeding into negative responses that will only imprison you into further misery.

The next chapter is about three significant game-changing leaders from Judah's tribe that directly resulted from Leah's praise. As I take Leah's focus to highlight these individuals, understand that to devote yourself to praise as Leah did, you must first understand the fruits of her praise.

If a rejected woman like Leah can find reasons to praise God, what does that tell you?

3

The Praise of Leah Echoes

> *But the Lord said to Samuel, "Do not consider his appearance or his height, for I have rejected him. The Lord does not look at the things people look at. People look at the outward appearance, but the Lord looks at the heart."*
> **1 Samuel 16:7**

Many individuals in the Bible had an outward appearance and status that did not fit the mass population's expectations. Society overlooks people who do not meet their visual expectations. But God uses these very individuals rejected by society to lead His ministry. For instance, when God was ready to replace King Saul, God instructed the prophet Samuel to go to Bethlehem to anoint the new king God had chosen.

Without knowing who the king would be, Samuel envisioned what this new king would look like. It was apparent that he expected this new leader would have the physical appearance to meet the social standards; he would be tall and muscular, with a chiseled jawline. This new king would probably resemble the 6'2" bodybuilding icon Arnold

Schwarzenegger from *The Terminator*. Perhaps the prophet envisioned this new king resembling the Greek demigod Hercules, who possessed superhuman strength and would fight off the intimating nations single-handedly.

So, Samuel went to Jessie's house to meet with his first son, Eliab. Samuel saw that Eliab had a king-like appearance. However, God had already rejected him. God confronted Samuel. Although Samuel was a faithful man of God who led a significant prophetic ministry, he could not help but be human, like so many of us.

We tend to judge others based on the superficial physical appearance we see with the naked eye, while God penetrates our being to evaluate our hearts. God chose David, the youngest son between twelve and sixteen, to replace King Saul (1 Samuel 16: 6-12). Repeatedly in the Bible, we see how our outward beauty and social status do not move God.

David was not Samuel's first choice, but God has a way of pouring out His blessings on those whose outward appearance looks unfit for the job but who have a devoted love for God. Like his ancestral mother, Leah, David would face discrimination because he lacked a king's appearance. But here, too, God would intervene.

In the life of David, we will see how Jacob's blessings were manifested in his ministry. Seven of Jesse's sons would be presented, yet God did not choose any of them. God had chosen the youngest, who was out back, tending the sheep. Samuel anointed the young boy with oil, and the "Spirit of the Lord came powerfully upon David" (1 Samuel 16:13). The Spirit of the Lord departed from King Saul (1 Samuel 16:14).

King David

"Who is this uncircumcised Philistine that he should defy the armies of the living God?"

1 Samuel 17:26

David was a man of many talents; he spoke well, and he was a brave man. Once again, David was underestimated because of his appearance.

David confronted Goliath, the Philistine's champion, who measured at "six cubits and a span." (1 Samuel 17:4)—about 9'9" if each cubit is 18 inches and a span is 9 inches. However, Goliath's size didn't seem to intimate the young shepherd. He only had his rod, five smooth stones, a pouch bag, and a sling (1 Samuel 17:44). Goliath thought it was some practical joke. He was intimidated by David, but David was not a bit intimidated by this incredible hulk.

David boldly told Goliath, "You come against me with sword and spear and javelin, but I come against you in the name of the Lord Almighty...and he will give all of you into our hands" (1 Samuel 17: 45-47). He killed Goliath with just one shot, fulfilling Jacob's prophecy to the Tribe of Judah. David received tremendous praise from the Israelites for his heroic victory.

David was a man of praise, responsible for many songs from the Book of Psalms. In them, we witness David's fiery passion for God and how he glorified Him. While transporting the Ark of the Covenant in the City of David, he "danced before the Lord with all his might," embarrassing his wife at the time (2 Samuel 6:14-16). King David was never a man who cared about what people thought of him. He was devoted to doing God's work, and that was all that mattered to him.

Despite all his accomplishments, David humbled himself before God through song, prayer, dance, and offerings. In turn, God blessed him tremendously through military victories. His reliance and unceasing pursuit of God's blessing is why David was a man after God's own heart. God promised that the rulership would remain in his descendants forever.

King Solomon

Leah's praise did not only come with royal kingship; she also attracted great wealth. Through her descendant, King Solomon, it is evident how one praise can impact future generations.

King Solomon, the son of King David, wasn't only wealthy like many others but had greater riches than all before him. His wealth in today's economy was no match for Warren Buffett. It even surpasses America's richest man, John D. Rockefeller, and his $663.4 billion net worth.

King Solomon accumulated wealth in various ways. Each year, King Solomon received 25 tons of gold (2 Chronicles 9: 13). One ton of gold is worth $64.3 million at $2000/oz. Researchers believe that his net worth was $2 trillion. This did not include the gifts he received from the guests, taxes from other nations, and money for trading efforts.

However, he was not a man of war like his father; he was very diplomatic, and no significant wars were recorded during his time. He formed commercial and political alliances with many neighboring lands, even powerful nations such as Egypt. Many unions included marriages with foreign wives, gaining him 700 wives and 300 concubines. As a result, all of Israel experienced large economic growth.

King Solomon was also known for his many building projects. These included the Forest of Lebanon, fleets of ships, harbors, stables for horses, and rebuilding several cities (1 Kings 7:1-12). Most importantly, he was the first to build the Temple of God in Jerusalem to house the Ark of the Covenant that King David prepared for him (1 Kings 6:1). The Temple of God was also lavish, built mainly of stone, with golden alter and other embellishments. His public service work included a well for the city's water source and trade expansion through a more efficient merchant fleet and tariff fees.

His daily living was luxurious. His throne was made of pure gold; the six stairs, twelve lion statues, and small stools used to support his feet were all gold. King Solomon's drinking cup and utensils were pure gold. In fact, silver wasn't even considered valuable in his day (1 Chronicles 9: 20). He was the richest and wisest of all the kings in the world during the Old Testament (1 Chronicle 9:22) and still wealthier and wiser than all the leaders in our modern time. He was a supreme leader from the Euphrates River to Philistia and the Egyptian border (1 Chronicle 9:27).

King Solomon was also famous throughout the lands for wisdom greater than any other king. His famous judgment regarding a dispute over verifying the birth mother of an infant child, a proposal to split the child in half, helped identify the actual mother because she was willing to lose her son rather than kill him (1 Kings 3:16-28).

The life of King Solomon demonstrates many reasons why Leah couldn't help but praise God. He lived an incredible life. To this day, King Solomon's wealth and wisdom are still recognized as one of the greatest in history. Like King Solomon, Leah was blessed beyond her imagination. Her blessing would always be talked about, even today.

Jehovah-Jireh is the God who provides. He is the giver of all gifts, blessings, and abundance. No one who puts their trust in the Lord is put to shame. He raises those who praise him. He showers them with wealth and prosperity beyond measure. Once He establishes a covenant with you, it is binding.

God demonstrated incredible prosperity through Leah's inheritance. In her time of rejection and misery, she gave birth to some of the greatest kings to ever rule. They received renown and recognition from other strong nations in their time, making their mark on ancient history with their strength and courage. Like Leah praised God, her sons would pursue God's heart. They paved the way for the King of Kings to make his entrance.

As Leah's praise blessed all the children of God, her praise immensely blessed you and me.

4

Leah Became the Bloodline of Jesus

From a shepherd boy to a royal king, reigning all over Israel and Judah in Jerusalem, David remained faithful to God. For that, God established an unconditional covenant with David. He promised him that from his lineage, the Messiah would establish his kingdom, which would last forever.

"Do not be afraid, Mary; you have found favor with God. ³¹ You will conceive and give birth to a son, and you are to call him Jesus. ³² He will be great and will be called the Son of the Most High. The Lord God will give him the throne of his father David, ³³, and he will reign over Jacob's descendants forever; his kingdom will never end."
Luke 1: 30-33

Something miraculous happened when Leah gave birth to her fourth son. Not only did she shift her focus from Jacob to the Lord, but Leah found favor in His eyes. Through the birth of Judea, He was fulfilling His promise to humankind.

The incredible thing about Judea is that Jacob was on one accord with Leah. Jacob blessed Judah and his descendants to take on the royal kingship role. Jacob prophesied over Judah that his brothers would praise and bow down to him and that the scepter and the ruler's rod, representing supreme authority, would not depart from Judah until he to whom it belonged came and established his authority.

The time had come for God to fulfill his promise.

Mary was a virgin woman from the tribe of Judah and a descendant of King David. She was engaged to Joseph when the angel Gabriel approached her with a message that would forever change her life.

Going about her daily routine, she had no idea she was chosen to carry such miraculous offspring. Mary was seen praising God through her pregnancy, similar to her ancestral mother, Leah. Mary was a humble and obedient woman of faith. She wasn't a queen or princess and had no fame or status, but she came from the House of David through David's son, Nathan, whose mother was Bathsheba. However, many families lost their wealth due to the Judahites' captivity in the Old Testament, explaining why Mary did not hold any status. Her miraculous pregnancy by the Holy Spirit with the Son of God baffled the young couple and the town.

We ought to praise God just because He is God. You cannot wait for everything to go well for you before you glorify God. Your praise matters the most during chaos, rejection, pain, and hurt. Leah praised God after the birth of her fourth child, Judah, from the depths of her heart. Her praise reached the heavens and created a ripple effect that would travel through the centuries until Jesus was born.

Praying and praising go in hand. Leah prayed to God, and although her situation never changed, she praised Him. When prayers go up, blessings come down. Therefore, praise is critical, no matter what your problem is.

Despite her circumstances, Leah's praise was pivotal in the Bible's history. Even after her death, we see that Leah's praise had a lasting effect that will penetrate through centuries, echoing God's magnificent authority over the Earth. Her praises' sound waves shifted the atmosphere forever, creating a continual reflection that will never end.

Jesus and Rejection

"The stone that the builders rejected has become the very head of the corner."

1 Peter 2:7

God chooses the least to rise to be the greatest. God raises those who are humble. Jesus was born king but the most modest king that would ever exist. His mother and stepfather were descendants of David but didn't inherit any royal status.

You would think this heavenly God would have made some special considerations. God, whose power is infinite, could have made a dramatic scene at the birth of Jesus to show the world that His son had arrived. God could have led an elaborate festival. However, God did the opposite.

I believe God loved Leah so much because he knew His son would also face rejection on Earth. Leah, a faithful woman of God, endured rejection from those she loved the most. First, as the oldest sister, her chances of marriage were very slim. Her father, whom she trusted, involved her in a scam. Then, the man she married didn't love her, no matter how hard she tried. The only sister she had was in a contest with her. It seemed like there was no hope for this poor woman, and she had no one to turn to for comfort.

Yet, when she prayed to God, He saw beauty in her that the world was too blind to see. God opened her womb and blessed her descendants. Her blessings were not only for a moment—they were eternal. God chose Leah, not Rachel, for his divine purpose as the ancestral mother of Jesus because Leah knew how to remain faithful amid rejection.

Rejection is a painful experience. It is unbearable when you offer your heart insincerity to someone, but they take it and stomp all over it while your heart is wailing for mercy. To watch the person or people you've invested all your affection in be indifferent, disinterested, or disloyal will make you feel abandoned.

Leah worked hard to prove herself capable and qualified as Jacob's loving wife. However, he did not seem to care any more than when he left her for Rachel. Leah could have been bitter or sour or walked around with a chip on her shoulder. In Leah's shoes, many of us would not have dealt with her rejection wisely. But Leah beat the odds. She kept hope alive, and she praised God. God must have looked down from Heaven with astonishment.

Jesus would be a faithful Son of God who would endure rejection by the very ones he loved and came to save. They would share the pain of rejection and obedience to God's word.

Jesus wasn't exactly what the Jews had in mind. Jesus wasn't born with a silver spoon in his mouth or served with a silver platter. Although Jesus's life was filled with blessings, he remained focused on his assignment ordained by God. Jesus faced numerous rejections but never let it derail him from fulfilling his destiny.

The Jews had created the image of what the Promised Messiah would resemble. He would behave in a certain way, affirm what they affirmed, and reject what they rejected. He would descend from Heaven on their terms, fighting against their enemies and restoring their Jewish nationalism on Earth.

However, Jesus didn't fit their superhero fantasy. Jews were under the Roman Empire's authority and hoped for a king to rescue them. They missed the prophecies of the suffering servant.

Jesus came to establish a relationship between His people and God. He embraced Israel's enemies with an entirely different doctrine. They raised eyebrows because of the company he was associated with. He hung out with the poor and the outcasts, people the religious fanatics would want nothing to do with. As a king, he didn't sit with the royal rod.

Jesus Rejected in His Hometown

> *They got up, drove him out of the town, and took him to the brow of the hill on which the town was built in order to throw him off the cliff.*
>
> **Luke 4:29**

Sometime after Jesus' baptism and his forty days and nights of fasting, Jesus went to the synagogue in his hometown. He read a famous Jewish passage from the Prophet Isaiah by identifying himself as the one spoken of by Isaiah. To the congregation, he appeared like an ordinary guy impersonating the Messiah.

Skepticism rose when Jesus revealed himself. The townspeople of Nazareth refused to believe that this poor carpenter's son, whom they watched grow up, could have the audacity to make such a bold proclamation. Jesus was not a rabbi, nor did he hold any religious office. In their narrow-minded understanding, it didn't make sense how Jesus could have such authority. They thought he was crazy. They became angry and attempted to kill Jesus by throwing him off a cliffside. However, he managed to escape the mob of furious townspeople.

Jesus Rejected by His Disciples

Peter was the most radical of Jesus's twelve disciples. Though he reassured Jesus that he was there for the long haul, Peter would soon deny Jesus three times before the rooster crowed, just as Jesus prophesized. Judas would later betray Jesus, leading to His crucifixion. Even among His most intimate comrades, Jesus was not safe.

The night before Jesus's arrest, He knew His death was near. Like any human being, He was nervous. This was the only time when Jesus was vulnerable. This time, He could not just get up and walk away. He brought a few selected disciples to pray with Him in Gethsemane, but they kept falling asleep. He woke them up, and they fell right back asleep. When Jesus was illegally arrested, all the disciples fled. The Man of God was left all alone. It was Jesus vs. the people—a game He would not win. Rejection had escalated to hatred and then murder.

Jesus experienced tremendous humiliation, excruciating torture, and dynamic execution. Even God rejected Jesus in the final hour.

Jesus was pinned to a rugged cross with a crown made of thorns. Bearing all the sins of the people, Jesus was the final sacrifice. Jesus became unrecognizable as the people's immense debaucheries and sins were transferred to the Son of God. He cried out in agony as he suffered the separation between Him and His father, "My God, My God, why have you forsaken me?" (Mark 15:34). His father, who knew no sin, could not exist where there was a sin. His earthly ministry would come to an end.

Jesus was not a cold-hearted Messiah. He was committed to the call and deeply invested in building relationships with the people. However, the people were not ready to embark on this new discipline.

Jesus had to conquer rejection because it would have hindered His ministry if He didn't. When the lies of rejection penetrate our minds, it sucks the life out of us. We become victims of mass destruction. Jesus encountered rejection many times in His life—it is inevitable. However, if you do not deal with it healthily, it will severely affect your well-being.

Facing rejection with maladaptive defense mechanisms festers emotional wounds that open us up to evil spirits. It distracts us from living a purposeful life and all God has created us to be. If you do not attack rejection with the word of God, the emotional wounds will swallow you up.

Rejection brings negative emotions: insecurity, worthlessness, vindictiveness, envy, and hate. However, Jesus was never vengeful. He asked for forgiveness for his transgressors on the cross.

Rejection feeds lies to you. It tells you that something must be wrong with you, that you are not good enough, not pretty enough. Rejection may say that nobody wants you while God is waiting to have a relationship with you. God loves you and cares for you. When you allow rejection to cloud your life, you have opened the door for Satan to manifest in your mind.

Satan is an accuser and uses rejection to imprison us, displacing our identity through insecurity. When Satan plants the seed of rejection in our lives, we become paralyzed in self-hatred if we fail to seek communion with God. Remember, Satan comes to kill, steal, and destroy. Jesus came so that we may have abundant life.

Someone with a rejected mentality is hypersensitive and fears being unwanted and unaccepted by others. You may begin to avoid future relationships, missing out on God's love for us. It makes emotional walls that separate us from the love of God, self-love, and the love of others.

Separation from God is dangerous. It begins with distrusting that God will come through for you. You doubt the goodness of God because, within these emotional walls, you cannot see beyond your hurt. We wallow in pain and allow Satan to fill our void. Satan is very strategic; he uses experiences from your past and replays them every time he wants to sabotage our relationships.

When you wallow in despair, you create space for Satan, and all his kinfolks make his home your mind. Before you know it, the feeling of rejection leads to depression. Untreated depression plucks out the hope that kept you grounded until you can't find a reason to live anymore. How you deal with rejection cannot be taken lightly. Jesus never allowed Satan to entice Him because He was steadfast in the word.

Do not expect to combat rejection with your strength. We are not equipped to fight it off alone—that is why prayer is so important. You may feel like you are the only one to face such an experience because rejection isolates you and makes you feel lonely. You are not alone. Remember that Jesus was a man of grief. He got rejected to the point of death. Do not just bury the experience, thinking that ignoring it will make it disappear because it gets stored in your subconscious. Use the word of God to throw your uppercut and jab punches at the enemy.

When you attempt to fight with your power alone, you open the gateway for Satan to have a field day because these are mighty dark forces battling against you. Therefore, you need greater strength to compete against the demonic forces of rejection. Do not think for a second about not making the cheerleading team because you were considered too chubby; Satan uses these past experiences against you, reminding you of the opportunities that you were denied.

I know these experiences were hurtful. If they weren't, they would not haunt you into your adulthood. However, you must not allow rejection to define you. Instead, view rejection as a way for God to elevate you. This requires that you surrender your will and your pride, but in this way, rejection can be a blessing.

If Jesus could not avoid rejection, then give up all avoidance ideas. Rejection happens. Coping with it healthily without allowing it to cripple you is a sign of maturity and strength. God's love is unconditional, and His everlasting love is plentiful.

Jesus Was Unattractive

He had no beauty or majesty to attract us to him, nothing in his appearance that we should desire him.

Isaiah 53: 2

Isaiah prophesized that the Messiah would be unattractive. Why would God create Jesus as an unattractive savior? We know that physical attractiveness is a crucial component in society, but God wanted the believers to follow Jesus without regard for his looks. He did not wish His handsome features to attract them but for them to follow Jesus because of God's word.

From earlier in this book, we know that we associate all physical attractiveness with good things. He already knew that we would fail to grasp the true gospel with our carnal judgment because we would be too busy admiring Him for his looks. Had Jesus resembled the famous 6'4" chiseled wrestler and actor Dwayne "The Rock" Johnson, He would not have had to say much to convince the crowd that He was the Son of God. All He would have to do was flex his pectoral muscles, and the public would be amazed. His dreamy eyes and honeycomb sermons would have swept the nation. The religious fanatics would have still challenged him, but His physique would have dominated the conversation. His spirit would have been seen shining through his body.

But that was not the case. Jesus was a man who was not physically attractive. Sound similar? Leah was unattractive. More and more, it seems like Leah's suffrage served a divine purpose. God chose Leah over Rachel not because He felt sorry for her but because He had a bigger plan for her and His kingdom. God saw that Leah was unloved, so he accepted, comforted, and loved her. Our God, the beginning and the end, knew that His only begotten son would experience the same discrimination and rejection on Earth.

Jesus did not meet the religious or social standards for beauty. He would have to be strong in the Lord and not allow outside pressure to interrupt the blessings on the inside. For that, Leah became the perfect woman for the job. God established a relationship with Leah and a lineage from which the Messiah would descend.

Leah and Jesus both fell prey to the grim reality of attractive discrimination. However, God would bless them with His glory.

5

How Jesus Dealt with Rejection

Even the Son of God experienced rejection. Jesus dealt with numerous pushbacks and challenges during his ministry on Earth, provoking the religious leaders and their stiff establishment. His new, unique covenant teachings intimidated political leaders and astonished the community and his family. Jesus was controversial and unapologetic about His messages, standing firm and not allowing His opponents to stand in the way of His father's assignment.

Jesus was teaching the "good news" in a fashion never taught before. Where better to start His ministry than in His hometown? After all, wouldn't they be excited that the Messiah came from among them? Knowing they were special would have given them bragging rights and a sense of pride.

However, the townspeople were blinded by their expectations. Their stubborn hearts were reluctant to accept the new covenant, stuck on the fact that they knew His parents, half-siblings, and upbringing. They were against His teachings because He didn't fit their standard of a Messiah.

Their lack of faith led Jesus to conclude that it was only in His hometown that a prophet was without honor. Since he got a lot of positive press in other cities, he soon stopped ministering in Nazareth.

Through his ministry life, He taught us how to thrive through rejection. Rejection from others can be discouraging, but it is not a dead end. After all, Jesus never sought approval. He was sure about who He was and His assignment on Earth.

Jesus didn't get paraded of love or popularity upon returning to Nazareth.

Jesus didn't quit His ministry when the townspeople labeled Him as mentally insane and attempted to throw him off a cliff.

Jesus didn't wrap his self-worth or identity around the approval of others.

Leah and Jesus both encountered rejection in their life. Their main difference is that Leah sought Jacob's approval while Jesus brushed off the rejection to remain focused on His assignment. We can learn many lessons by examining how Jesus dealt with rejection and the differences between Him and Leah.

For example, Jesus focused on demonstrating love, while Leah focused on receiving love. Jesus taught His Father's love; He was kind to the outcasts. He came down to establish a new covenant with the people. He shared His love with the least likely, such as the Samaritan woman. He did not focus on receiving approval from anyone.

In Leah's life, we see that focusing on the approval of others will leave you empty. It will never fill the void inside you, like pouring water into a cracked vase. The only way to break that cycle is to take on God's yoke and give Him your heavy burden. God wants you to provide him with your heartaches and pain. Learn to focus on what God says about you and who God has created you to be.

When validation is dependent on external factors, like circumstances or people, it can negatively impact our mental health because external validation brings fear. We fear what others will think about us if we say the wrong thing or do not live up to social expectations. Focusing on God's words is the only way to build healthier boundaries.

Jesus read the Word of God, prayed, and fasted. He spent time with God, even though He was the Son of God.

You can do that too!

To resist the challenges of rejection, you must pray and read scriptures to restore your faith and build self-reliance. This consistent practice will strengthen your internal validation and suffocate approval addiction.

Jesus demonstrated how to deal with rejection because He was not a conformist. Jesus didn't change His message to get the approval of the townspeople, family, or leaders. He knew the trend but chose not to adapt since it did not coincide with His father's plans. He didn't stress that He was hated and that they were out to kill Him.

Jesus's response to rejection teaches us how to respond when facing rejection in our own lives. We all want to feel accepted; it's human nature. However, it's a problem when you depend strongly on others' approval to determine your self-worth. Doing things intentionally solely to receive praise and recognition will lead to disappointment. It is self-sabotaging when you rely on how many "likes" and "followers" on social media but lack healthy social boundaries.

Be aware of even the smallest thoughts you allow to penetrate your mind. They may start small but soon metastasize uncontrollably into cancer, which kills all your confidence. Approval addiction is a blood-sucking parasite that will only leave you empty and lonely in the end. You stay too long in bad situations or relationships because you put too much energy into convincing them to accept you. Like any addiction, you will never be satisfied. You will always want more and more to get the same high.

Ending approval addiction is the beginning of freedom because we are no longer enslaved to others' opinions. For some folks, they will not change their minds about you no matter what you do, even if you cross the ocean or jump over the moon for them. I know it doesn't happen overnight and requires much internal work. But that is where prayer becomes handy.

Jesus sought God, and He knew the word. Whenever the chief priest, scribes, or any religious leader would challenge His authority, He always had a comeback. He never allowed their belittling to intimidate His God-given divinity.

As the Son of God, it did not exempt Him from the scheme of Satan. Satan waited until Jesus was alone and vulnerable to make his move, manipulating the word of God to deceive Him. He resisted because He was devoted to praying. It is essential to know that Satan will aim to destroy you from a familiar place, using issues closest to your heart. Prayer is our weapon. If folks do not like you, don't beg them to like you. Just keep it moving.

Close people in your circle may disapprove of you because they know where you came from, what you did, past failures, and so on. We saw it happen during Jesus's ministry on Earth. Please do not let it discourage you, although it is challenging. Do not let the disapproval or rejection of others pull you down. Holding on to these things will prevent you from moving forward, and God is getting ready to do something new in your life.

If you meditate on the word of God and seek guidance from Him, He will direct your path. Maybe you were overlooked because you were not of the right age group, ethnicity, or status. It may seem like a roadblock. It is okay; I believe we all have been through this experience at least once. What is important is how we respond, which will determine the outcome.

Spend time with the Lord, and you will not be disappointed. Sometimes, He allows others to reject you for you to see their true intentions. Jesus experienced the paparazzi, the numerous followers whose hearts were not after God. They came in masses and left in masses. They walked away from Jesus when His teaching did not benefit their agenda. However, Jesus remained steadfast in his assignment and loyalty to God. He never chased after them or begged them to come back.

We do not see Jesus apologetic for preaching the gospel. We never read that he changed His message to earn "likes" from the people. Jesus boldly declared the word of God, and that message was new and unique.

Although He preached spirituality to the masses, many were not ready to be committed to the call, so they rejected Jesus. He turned to the twelve disciples and asked them if they wanted to join the followers who had left Him.

6

Leah's Honorable Burial

When Rachel saw that she was not bearing Jacob any children, she became jealous of her sister. So she said to Jacob, "Give me children, or I'll die!"
Genesis 30: 1

Beauty does not exempt one from a pain-free life. Rachel can attest to that. She was swept off her feet by Jacob's love. Perhaps Rachel thought that she would live happily ever after. After all, Rachel had both beauty and love on her side. What more could she ever ask for?

The sad truth was that she still found discontent despite Jacob's abundant love. The feeling of something lacking, thoughts of missed opportunities, and unrealized potential can even exist for those like Rachel.

Watching Leah praise God with her sons provoked jealousy in Rachel's heart. Jealousy is an ugly emotion that hinders us from experiencing God's love. Though Rachel was outwardly beautiful, inwardly, she was in a contest with her sister.

She was obsessed with having children and convinced that life was not worth living if she did not. She blamed her husband, demanding that Jacob give her children or else she would die. Her demand must have struck Jacob's ego because as much as Jacob loved Rachel, his response was fierce. He rebuked Rachel for blaming him while her barrenness was from God.

Rachel allowed her preoccupation with her barrenness to drive her insane. When Ruben found some mandrake from the field and brought it to Leah, Rachel noticed it and demanded to have it. The mandrake was considered a fertile root that would grant her what she wanted the most. Unfortunately, it was not effective.

Ultimately, God answered Rachel's prayer and gave her a son. She named him Joseph, meaning for God to add another son. Rachel's quest for motherhood was to compete against her sister; even her children's names were in reference to this rivalry. Therefore, one child was not enough. To stay in the race with a winning chance, she needed more.

At her request, she became pregnant again. Things were looking right at first. Unfortunately, it would not end well for Rachel. She died during childbirth with her son Benjamin. On her last breath, she named him Ben-oni, "son of my suffering." Jacob later changed his name to Benjamin, "son of my right hand."

Rachel died while in the contest with her sister, leaving behind Jacob and her two sons. She was buried on the wayside in Bethlehem.

Did her jealousy lead to her tragic death? Only God knows. The Bible tells us that Rachel committed adultery because she stole her father's idols when God instructed Jacob to leave Laban's estate. She then lied about it when Laban came looking for them. Not knowing that Rachel was the culprit, Joseph declared that whoever stole the idols would surely die. Perhaps her premature death was due to the curse brought on herself.

But, the rivalry between her and her sister undoubtedly prevented her from experiencing God's love. She never got the chance to thank God for her bundle of joy; she was busy focusing on her lack.

Do you spend too much time focusing on what you don't have in your life? If you do, I challenge you to praise God for what He has done for you instead of indulging in jealousy or bitterness. It's not worth the energy.

Both sisters had their faults, but Leah took a different approach that was deemed remarkable. The Bible stressed where Leah's blessing came from, as she relied on God's love for security. It was not easy for Leah, nor is it for any of us.

After Rachel died, the Bible does not tell us how many years Jacob and Leah spent together nor about their relationship. Surprisingly, Leah, whom Jacob did not love, rested alongside Jacob in her grave.

Although Leah could not change Jacob's heart, she transformed herself and her focus. She saw that the hand of God was on her and did not take it for granted. God gave her significance when she was rejected. Leah was grateful for what God gave her. She experienced an abundant life through her faith, resting in His glory.

In the End, Leah is Honored

...Bury me with my fathers in the cave in the field of Ephron the Hittite, 30 ... 31 There Abraham and his wife Sarah were buried, there Isaac and his wife Rebekah were buried, and there I buried Leah.
Genesis 49:29-31

Jacob indeed honored Leah in death. Before Jacob's death, he gave clear instructions regarding his burial arrangement. Leah was already buried there with his ancestors. The burial place was significant because it represented God's promise of the Land.

In Genesis's book, God promised Abraham that his descendants would possess the land where Abraham was buried. The cave of Machpelah was his family's real estate, purchased by Abraham from the Hittites. Therefore, Jacob needed to be buried in the Promised Land, Canaan, where his tomb would signify his faith in God's promise. His grandfather, Abraham, and his father, Isaac, were already buried there with their wives. Jacob would be the third generation to be buried with his wife.

Through her devotion to God, Leah was the wife picked to rest with God's chosen family. Traditionally, to be buried alongside family members signified your love and loyalty, and it was an honor to be buried in a designated family plot—a common practice among royal and wealthy families.

Although he was living in Egypt at the time of his death due to the harsh famine, Jacob knew Egypt was not the Promised Land. Canaan, where he was born, raised, and buried, was the home of future kingdoms.

Why did Jacob choose Leah to rest with his family?

Although Rachel's death was sudden, ensuring that Rachel was buried with his ancestors would have been no hassle for Jacob. Remember, he worked fourteen years to get her hand in marriage.

In the end, Jacob, who also underwent his own spiritual journey, became spiritually mature enough to discern that Leah was God's blessing. Leah's sons made up half the tribe of Israel, dominating the tribe. He spent so much time pursuing his fleshly desire when he needed Leah to accomplish God's promise to Abraham. Lust limited Jacob's perception of beauty.

This is not to say that physical attractiveness is evil. However, focusing on physical beauty or worldly things to satisfy you will provide temporary pleasure. But what happens when that pleasure fades out? Some things in life cannot be bought.

And so, Jacob chose Leah over Rachel to rest alongside him and his family. Perhaps it could be that Jacob began to see God's love radiating through Leah and realized she was aligned with God's will. Though Leah lacked outward beauty, she possessed inward beauty and was more righteous than Rachel.

Do not get me wrong, Jacob loved Rachel till death separated them. Although she was barren throughout most of their marriage, Jacob never stopped loving her. But this twist in their story demonstrates how God rewards those who diligently seek Him. During Leah's suffering, she did not become bitter or hateful toward God or any parties involved. She was very hopeful. She had her shortcomings through her quest to win Jacob's heart, but God's love covered her during her weak moments.

The true love story was between Leah and God.

7

Self-Image

The obsession with physical beauty is more persuasive than ever due to the evolution of mobile technology and social media sites, particularly for the millennials—individuals born between 1981 and 1997. Because Instagram is more of an image-based social platform than the combination of written text and images of social media found on Facebook and Twitter, Instagram is the most detrimental cause of body dissatisfaction in women.

Generally, social media platforms are prominent in our everyday lives. While this is a great way to stay connected with friends and loved ones, constantly viewing Photoshopped images of idealized beauty can increase the chances of our body dissatisfaction.

Unlike traditional broadcast media, such as the television and magazine models that Generation X experienced, social media is interactive and more accessible. You no longer must wait to go to the grocery store to find magazines of thin models or turn on the television when you get home from work as the previous generation did before the internet boom. Celebrities and models are accessible every second of the day on your smartphone. They use relational communication strategies and possess a more identity-based platform that allows individuals to display their unique selves in a body-centric manner.

For example, Instagram users can take pictures or selfies and self-portrait-style photographs and post them on their page. This immediate and constant reminder of others' curated images makes us more susceptible to increased self-hatred dangers.

The Cost of Beauty

According to the Pew Research Center (2018), 76% of Instagram users visit the site daily, with 60% reporting that they do so several times per day.

Instagram, which began in 2010, quickly gained popularity by garnering over 500 million active monthly users who shared 95 million photos daily by June 2016 (Wagner, 2016). The hype and intriguing frequent use of social media caused many millennials to become more invested in creating an idealized image accepted by the online world (Wagner, as cited in Gonzales and Hancock, 2011). Physical appearance influences the attention and traffic one receives with every social media post. Because of this, many individuals use appearance-changing strategies to attract followers, likes, and comments.

There are different levels of such a process. One may make minor changes to their appearance, such as wearing makeup or more revealing clothing. However, there are more dramatic and permanent changes, such as plastic surgery. Increased social media use correlates with appearance comparison and internalization, particularly millennials and Gen Z. The more a person continuously views attractive celebrities and peers, the more it affects their self-esteem and perception of self-worth.

As viewers, we crave to experience this newfound happiness through physical perfection. One may think that a little tweak here and there will resolve their problem. However, many do not realize that celebrities make up a more extensive social media campaign that uses algorithms to help companies sort out the best influencers for their brand audience (Forbes, 2016).

It is a marketing strategy that is highly effective and subtle because people generally learn behaviors through examples. So, by psychologically manipulating our reasoning through observation, people are conditioned to new patterns of behaviors that appear to have surfaced from authentic relationships built during their digital interactions. This engagement promotes trust-building, attracting consumers into buying their products and services. Promoting idealized physical attractiveness leads to greater body dissatisfaction and willingness to have cosmetic surgeries.

Physical attractiveness is a highly valued commodity and is considered a significant asset for women. Physical beauty comes with an overwhelming advantage, protecting many individuals from society's undesirable consequences. Leah was victimized for a physical imperfection that she had little to no control over. Unfortunately for Leah, it was an era where cosmetic advancement had not yet been discovered.

Social tendencies to judge others by their physical appearance are damaging even beyond the social implications. Victims of appearance discrimination endure unfair stereotypes and assumptions. Unlike their more attractive counterparts, they are less likely to find employment, get promotions, marry, or continue their education (Adamitis, 2000).

To pour salt in their wound, many times, a cycle of discrimination will continue if the next generation continues to possess a similar dissatisfactory physical appearance. Women are more likely to experience appearance discrimination, resulting in economic and social disparity compared to men. Therefore, there is more significant pressure for women to participate in attractiveness enhancement regimens to increase their social acceptance opportunities.

8

The Perception of Beauty is Subjective

I praise you because I am fearfully and wonderfully made; your works are wonderful. I know that full well.
Psalms 139:14

Our perception of beauty is skewed and differs from person to person. Beauty is poorly defined and not thoroughly understood; beauty is alluring, seductive, attractive, sparks passion, and kindles happiness. Beauty standards vary worldwide and over the years, and people often value beauty more than virtue.

Confucius, a Chinese philosopher of the sixth century who taught a lot about moral wisdom, said that "everything has beauty, but not everyone sees it." I agree beauty is everywhere because everything that God created is beautiful. But we don't see it because we have preconceived notions about beauty. Beauty is constant, but perception is the variable. Perception depends on our likes and dislikes; what may appeal to one person may not be remotely appealing to another. Therefore, beauty is whatever we say it is.

The definition of beauty is tied to our own bias and culture. The natural beauty in God's creation is found in our outer appearance and the world around us. Beauty is infinite. Unfortunately, we take the indescribable aspect of beauty for granted and put such wisdom in a box to fit our limitations and insecurities. Beauty was never meant to be that simple; it should be unlimited and diverse, as complexity is captivating and mesmerizing. Perception attacks the comprehension of beauty to find itself depleted from lack of vision, and the true essence of beauty is misunderstood and misinterpreted.

Do not believe everything you see in the media. Companies try to sell the idea of beauty for their interest. For instance, Victoria's Secret displays its thin models to condition our minds on their definition of beauty. The celebrity or model you see posing on the front of a magazine is not posing in her natural beauty. These images have been altered through Photoshop or cosmetic surgeries. Many of these images are not even humanly possible—they were manufactured.

While many women think beauty is found in human-made products and embellishments, our beauty lies within our natural selves. As a woman, you must own your natural beauty. Understand that comparing yourself to other women weakens your ability to be unique. It forces you to chase an illusion, abandoning your value. There is power in being who God created you to be, not in imitating someone else. We should not be afraid to be different. It does not matter if you wear a size 2 or 22 or have full or thin lips. You are beautiful because God created you.

Although beauty plays a role in human relationships, it is widely accepted in Godly relationships. Beauty is not only skin deep but is found in our laughter, attitudes, and love for others. Correlating perfectional physical beauty to happiness and goodness is self-sabotaging. Blaming our insecurities on our perceived lack of beauty harms our well-being. Our creator didn't create assembly-line Barbie dolls because he wanted us to be different.

Society's beauty standards are not universal or permanent. Rather, they are like waves washing up on the seashore of culture and societal norms. They come swiftly and brainwash us before rushing back into the ocean.

Through the centuries, beauty standards have varied. Traditional practices were the norm in certain regions for only a period before being replaced by other customs. Political and affluent individuals usually had the most significant influence on how beauty was determined and what was acceptable. It didn't matter how hazardous or ridiculous a beauty standard may appear; if it was trendy, it was desirable.

Renaissance Curves

During the Italian Renaissance (1350-1600), full-figured women were considered beautiful, representing the ability to bear children and virtue. Other features like blonde curls, high foreheads, and round stomachs were all desirable. Women used time-consuming bleaching processes, damaging their hair in order to meet such standards. They also shaved their hairlines to get the desired effect and embraced plus-size figures.

That's right: women were glorified for being full-figured!

Dieting and fat-shaming did not exist during this era. The media would portray ideal beauty standards through artwork, poetry, and literature. To demonstrate wealth (which is always attractive), they would have to show signs of abundance; therefore, plus-size women with soft round bellies were considered beautiful because they could afford expensive food and did not perform manual labor, instead staying indoors to enjoy fine food. The working-class women were slimmer because they had to budget to not run out of food.

Japanese Smile

In the 19th century, Japanese women intentionally stained their teeth with black dye through a practice called Ohaguro, a strange yet widespread beauty custom associated with Japan. This traditional dental custom is the opposite of the contemporary North American straight and white teeth ideals.

Instead of whitening productions like Crest Whitestrips, the conventional method involved ingesting harsh dye with ingredients, including iron filings and pharmacological substances with high antimicrobial activity. It was an attractive beauty enhancement, prophylaxis for dental decay, and treatment for nasty tooth conditions (Khalid and Quinonez, 2015). Ohaguro was practiced by married women, single women, and prostitutes to signify their sexual maturity during the Edo period (1603-1863) (Smith, 2003, as cited by Khalid and Quinonez, 2015).

Black teeth were associated with royalty because sugar was an expensive commodity, and only individuals with affluence could afford sugary treats in the Renaissance, such as Queen Elizabeth I (Khalid and Quinonez, 2015). The influence of dental appearance is tied to society's fascination with beautiful smiles, overall physical attractiveness, and universal fertility indicators.

Selective beauty distinctions pose pressure for cosmetic enhancements and beauty reforms. Modifications to teeth are closely linked to society's idea that specific characteristics add value to beauty and status; therefore, they are worth achieving.

Elizabethan White Skin

In England, during the Elizabethan era in the 1500s, the highest standard of beauty was full-face white lead-based powder, a toxic skin-whitening method known as ceruse. The white-as-snow facial complexion signified wealth and nobility since poor people had to work outside and experienced tan complexions from sun exposure. It also helped to hide women's scars from smallpox and wrinkles. The paler a woman, the more attractive and feminine she was considered.

Renaissance-era women desired rosy cheeks and red lipsticks. They also regarded high foreheads to be nobler. Therefore, they would pluck out hair from their hairline. In addition, they desired a straight and narrow nose and arched brows—features that resembled Queen Elizabeth.

1920s Charleston Dancers

In contemporary culture, flat stomachs and large breasts and buttocks are ideal. In the 1920s, flapper fashion brought on a new standard of beauty in America. Boyish builds, flat chests, long legs, and short bob hairstyles were the new beauty standard. In addition, women adopted lightweight, single-layer short dresses and loose blouses, exposing cleavage. Women cut their hair and wore bras to give them that flat-chest look.

They were lively American girls who challenged images of domesticated women and noblewomen. They replaced the extremely long skirts with short ones rising over the knee, an essential fashion trait that would continue to exist. The corset worn during the Victorian era was seen as an object of suppression, so it was rejected, freeing women from the rigid undergarments. Women smoking and drinking were considered attractive, and drinking allowed women to easily enjoy social and relationship activities, releasing them from the Victorian era's ideologies.

Their simplicity, uniqueness, and unconventional behavior made headlines in the media. They were often featured in movies, newspapers, and magazines. Their fashion was found in popular articles such as Sears catalogs. Jazz music and Charleston dancing were popular, unlike the waltz from the Victorian era. The flappers were pioneers of a new way of life for women.

Egyptian Golden Beauty

Ancient Egypt is known for its unique cosmetology. They went to great lengths to emphasize their appearance and are credited with many cosmetic inventions. Eye makeup is likely the most captivating characteristic of their cosmetic line, dating back thousands of years before Christ. They used thick black eyeliner and colorful eyeshadow to outline their eyes in almond shapes with long-tailed corners. The most popular eyeshadow color was green, made from malachite. They wore lipstick, elaborate wigs, and jewelry.

Makeup not only enhanced their beauty but also had ritual significance and cultural meanings. They wore wigs to protect their scalp from the sun and head lice. Some women shaved off their hair to add full hair wigs while others added extensions. Many were seen with braids.

Several Ancient Egyptian beauty regimens are still seen today. They used henna dye to remove gray hair and paint their nails, waxed their body hair with honey and sugar, and wore high-quality perfumes. They prized "golden" complexions, unlike other cultures that preferred pale or white faces. Egyptians used bronzers mixed with cream to create their foundations instead of white lead. Oils and creams helped protect against the hot and dry climate and sandy winds by keeping the skin soft and preventing cracks— Cleopatra would indulge in milk baths to keep her skin rich and healthy. They loved the youthful look and had anti-wrinkle creams that included crocodile dung in their ingredients.

Even in death, the appearance was critical. They would prepare the skin and beautify the face before burial, taking many beauty tools to the grave. They believed in keeping an attractive physical appearance, even in the afterlife.

Padaung Elongated Neck

Natural beauty is based on our anatomy, but self-decoration with accessories enhances our beauty and symbolizes attractiveness and tribal identity.

Imagine stacks of brass rings coiled around the neck, a traditional ancient custom preserved to this day. The women from the Padaung Tribe in Thailand would begin wearing such metal from childhood until adulthood, initially increasing the number of rings, weighing from 4.5 pounds as a child to 22 pounds as an adult. The rings would create a visual illusion of lengthening their neck by pressing down their collarbone. This distinctive look gave them the "giraffe-neck" impression. It was uncomfortable yet widely practiced because it signified beauty to the tribe.

African Wooden Decoration.

Body piercing is a common practice worldwide that goes back to ancient times. Small piercings are widely seen in women, but the stretching of the earlobes is a unique cultural sign of beauty. Several cultures, such as the Maasai of Kenya and Tanzania, Mursi of Ethiopia, and West African Fulani women, artificially modify their earlobes' cartilage to fit large round wooden decorations to achieve Kenyan social beauty standards. They gradually mutilate their ear with stone or wood to demonstrate their strength and loyalty to their tribe, signifying womanhood.

Wearing a lip plate—a decorated flat disc inserted in the stretched-out lower center of the lip—is another unique beauty practice. Mursi tribe women located in the Southwest of Ethiopia would undergo gauging, the delicate process of stretching the lip. Initially, with a small incision of 2 to 4 cm, the lip plate gradually increases in size over time to a 10 to 15 cm diameter. This process takes several months to a year to complete without tearing the lips, which would ruin the entire process. A lip mutation forces women to extract between two to four bottom teeth to accommodate larger lip plates. Even if the woman removed the lip plate later, they would never restore their original shape.

It is a facial art performed by the girl's mother once she hits puberty, expressing the female maturity of childbearing age and marriage eligibility. Wearing the plate can be painful, making it difficult to speak, so they only wear them in the presence of men or during special ceremonies.

These women associate self-worth and strength with this tradition, providing social acceptance while increasing self-esteem and power in their communities; women who fail to wear lip plate are considered inferior to those who adhere to their ethnic practices. The more artistic a woman is with her body, the more attractive they are to the men they try to impress.

Modern Society and the Hourglass Figure

Today, we live in a society that perceives curvy hourglass figures as beautiful. Unlike the Italian Renaissance era, round stomachs are no longer perceived as attractive. Flat stomachs and large breasts, hips, and butts are considered beautiful.

With the help of plastic surgeons, if you don't like it, you can fix it. The negative stigmatism that cosmetic surgeries were once associated with is now widely reduced and exploited by celebrities worshiped for their youthful and idealized attractiveness. In 2014, 17.2% of millennials performed cosmetic surgeries to maintain, restore, or enhance their physical appearance. In 2017, there was a 1% increase in cosmetic surgeries performed (American Society for Aesthetic Plastic Surgery 2017, as cited in Walker et al. 2019). Due to social media's frequent usage, there is an intense desire for cosmetic surgeries, and these numbers will continue to climb.

The American Society of Plastic Surgeons (ASPS) is the world's largest organization of board-certified plastic surgeons, founded in 1931. It dominates the field with 93% of all board-certified plastic surgeons in the United States. According to the ASPS, 15.1 million cosmetic surgery procedures were performed in the United States in 2013, and more than 12 billion dollars were spent in 2014. The top five standard cosmetic surgical procedures performed are liposuction, breast augmentation, eyelid surgery, tummy tuck, and rhinoplasty (Jung and Hwang, 2016).

Beauty was the fourth-leading industry in 2014, with the most extensive reach of influencers in the United States (Forbes as cited in Statista, n.d). This is due to the increased pressure from contemporary societies, increased promotion from mass media to accept cosmetic surgery as a remedy for physical imperfections, and consumers connecting with peers (Forbes, 2016).

Celebrities are social influencers, a type of third-party endorser able to transform and control the viewer's behavior (Forbes as cited by Freberg, Graham, & McGaughey, 2010). Through her public engagement with cosmetic surgeries, *Keeping Up with the Kardashians* reality TV star Kim Kardashian increased the number of buttocks augmentations by 86% in 2014 (Jung and Hwang, 2016). Like many other reality stars and celebrities, Kim Kardashian gains the viewer's trust by allowing their followers access to their personal experiences and narratives. Influencers use these strategies to leverage their brand and express their unique selves. They are considered relatable and credible because they can promote physical attractiveness in a highly personalized way by sharing their opinion and personal journeys. They often reveal before and after pictures, creating an "ah-ha" moment. After their transformation, they demonstrate a boost of confidence to convince the viewers by posting glamorous photos of themselves being happy and satisfied with the new change.

This form of "monkey see monkey do" mentality leads many women to the desire to emulate the ideal media and society's attractiveness standards. Unfortunately, this curvy, hourglass figure is not naturally attainable for most women, forcing them to turn to cosmetic procedures.

9

I am Beautiful

It is essential to be aware that social media, television, magazines, and billboards do not always reflect reality. It is also necessary to be mindful of the dangers of appearance comparison. Doing so will promote the positive usage of social media. Sometimes, it will not hurt to unfollow pages that trigger negative self-thinking.

In our society and social media, size matters! Someone slim is considered socially acceptable. However, being overweight is deemed lazy and lacking in self-discipline (Dakanalis and Riva, 2013). Our society's pressure leads to "body shaming," imposing negative feelings about one's body due to weight (Dakanalis and Riva, 2013).

Body shaming has serious consequences. It leads to body obsession, comparison, and eating disorders. Victims of body shaming often develop psychological disorders such as depression, anxiety, eating disorders, and suicide. The higher the BMI, the greater the discrimination and stigmatization. When you have thin women as celebrities or models, it conditions women to believe that in order to be successful, desirable, or happy, one must achieve the media's ideal beauty and thinness.

The weight loss industry preys on body shaming victims by promising to rapidly transform their bodies into society's ideal of thinness. According to Marketdata, in 2017, people spent an estimated $64.9 billion in the U.S. in the commercial weight loss industry. An estimated 201,000 bariatric surgeries were performed in the US in 2016. Online dieting websites were worth an estimated $900 million, with WeightWatchers.com leading at $349 million. Companies such as Herbalife posted strong growth with meal replacements. The market was worth $4.16 billion.

Due to the increasing focus on weight loss, these companies have much to gain. For some people, no matter how they try, they regain the weight. Some even gain back more than they lost. When weight loss fails, it means repeat consumers.

Meanwhile, these individuals build guilt and self-hatred. These companies give the impression that success is guaranteed but fail to emphasize the necessity of long-term maintenance to stay thin. Many women become preoccupied with dieting and weight loss because society tells them that they are not good enough, pouring more money into the weight loss industry.

Ultra-thin models become the point of reference for some women who internalize repeated portrayals of what marketers aim to demonstrate as reality, and they tie their self-worth to society's weight scale. Social media and advertisements make us believe a woman's worth is based on her appearance. Therefore, a woman's value is diminished when her appearance and body do not meet society's expectations.

Marketers are in the business of making money, so they refuse to use average-size women because we will not invest in their useless products and services if we are confident with our bodies. They are willing to do almost anything to convince the population that they desperately need self-image improvement, even for the sake of portraying unrealistic thinness to body shame those on the opposite end of the spectrum. Beauty diversity and self-satisfaction do not lead to profit. Instead, the weight loss and beauty industry earns its money on the back of our insecurity and body dissatisfaction.

No two bodies are alike. We come in all shapes, curves, and sizes. In the media, all the models are identical. The way you view yourself is critical because it affects your mental health. If you believe that you are unworthy of being desired, it will lead to psychological distress, lower quality of life, and unhealthy eating behaviors. Greater body satisfaction and appreciation lead to greater well-being and a better quality of life.

Unconventional Beauty

According to Dove's 2010 global survey, 96% of women do not consider themselves beautiful—evidence that more women than we think are struggling with body image; about 672 million women globally. Not only is the statistic shocking, but it brings to light the elephant in the room. Suppose only 4% of women consider themselves beautiful worldwide despite all the beauty and cosmetic regimens available. In that case, this proves that it is not about a lack of beauty enhancement but a lack of self-esteem due to society's pressure to look a certain way.

Conventional beauty is the classification of beauty standards presented by society and/or social media, stating that women are considered beautiful only when they have these specific physical characteristics. The absence or lack of standardized features excludes a woman from being considered beautiful. This concept is destructive because it normalizes unrealistic expectations and puts pressure on women to meet impossible or difficult beauty standards. Many of these women are editing and photoshopping their bodies and faces to promote the illusion of ideal beauty.

Unconventional beauty widens the view of beauty, allowing women to be inclusively beautiful, not just a selected few. Unconventional beauty is diverse, not limited to one's complexion, hair texture, height, or body shape. Unconventional beauty redefines society's standards.

It enables women to perceive themselves positively while removing beauty insecurity and anxiety.

Plus-Size Matters!

"Nobody can make you feel inferior without your consent."

- Elanor Roosevelt

Changing the media's portrayal of women takes national and international effort. But some companies have joined that effort. The average American woman wears a size 14. Plus-size is classified as sizes between 14 to 34, accounting for 67% of the American female population. However, only an estimated 15% of the market comes to plus-size clothing.

This is an outrageous imbalance and neglect by the fashion industry. For too long, designers focused on the smallest size models that were unrealistically thin versus the mass population. However, the plus-size community is speaking up.

Lane Bryant, the first plus-size retailer, started in the early 1900s, is known for its century-long clothing designs and advocacy catered exclusively to women who require plus-size attires. Their campaign has always promoted body acceptance, such as the #PlusIsEqual and #ImNoAngel hashtags. They aim to represent 67% of the average-sized women overlooked and neglected for far too long by the media, confronting the delusion that destroyed so many women's confidence and balancing equality for all women.

Lane Bryant has made significant contributions to the plus-size community, successfully changing the conversation about beauty standards and teaching women to love their curves. Their movement shifted the fashion industry by allowing plus-size fashion to be part of the big picture, supporting events such as Full-Figured Fashion Week. Their #ImNoAngel campaign offers an alternative to lingerie's ultra-thin Victoria's Secret models. This is a bold move, considering that Victoria's Secret is the nation's largest and most popular lingerie company.

The difference between stumbling blocks and stepping stones depends on your perception. Challenges allow us to build a new reality and make history. Society will throw situations at you to debilitate your worth. However, it is up to you to decide if you will accept the lies that society tries to shove down your throat or stand up for yourself. It is not what they say about you that matters; how you respond makes a world of difference.

Plus-sized model Ashley Graham, among many others, is breaking the cycle of body shaming and self-hate, a tremendous breakthrough in the fashion world. Ashley Graham was the first plus-size model to be featured on the cover of *Sports Illustrated*'s annual swimsuit issue in 2016, showing off her size 16 voluptuous curves and triple-D chest. However, instead of wearing the typical one-piece suit, she wore a tiny bikini. This message was geared to overthrow the myth that plus-size women are too concerned with concealing their bodies and not interested in fashion or revealing their curves. The magazine cover encourages women of all sizes to believe that their curves are sexy enough to wear a bikini at the beach or pool.

Ashley Graham later appeared as a judge on *America's Next Top Model*, working alongside former Victoria's Secret model Tyra Banks. Ashley Graham was also the first-ever plus-size model to appear on the American *Vogue* magazine cover alongside Kendall Jenner and many others. This did not happen overnight, and there is still a lot of progress to be made. However, it is a step in the right direction.

Disabled Models

"Be the change that you want to see."
– Mahatma Gandhi

Women with physical disabilities can experience greater body dissatisfaction because they are often perceived as abnormal. These individuals are often excluded and underrepresented because they do not meet Western civilization's physical attractiveness standards. They receive higher stigmatization due to their physical differences, leading to social isolation and poor self-esteem.

Beauty diversity includes those with a physical disability. Someone with Down Syndrome, missing limbs, or visual and hearing impairments is commonly neglected by the fashion, beauty, and media industries. It is almost as if the disabled population does not exist or that beauty and disability are mutually exclusive. Finding fashion for someone with physical limitations can be very challenging.

Lately, several disabled individuals and organizations have made it their mission to change the social perception of beauty by showcasing individuals with various physical disabilities to the fashion industry and providing women with a way to positively identify with their disability on the same social platform as the non-disabled. Visual reinforcement by social institutions is a strong influencer in our society—the media conditions our attitude and perception of social acceptance, desirability, and understanding. By embracing disabled models, media outlets raise awareness and provide greater social acceptance. Disabled designers created a fashion line for those with physical limitations by creating exclusively adaptive clothing to meet their needs.

Clothing is an essential aspect of how our physical appearance is portrayed in society, fostering a sense of belonging to specific social groups or norms. Clothing and fashion enhance self-confidence and promote personal identity. That is why apparel is a multi-billion-dollar industry. You are expected to meet apparel standards in every setting and occasion. However, most retailers do not realize that conventional clothing will likely pose a challenge for someone with functional limitations.

Adaptive clothing is not simple to design. It takes a team of occupational therapists and human engineers to consult fashion designers to design clothing with special modifications. Due to variations in body features and functions, it is a complicated yet fulfilling endeavor. People with disabilities deserve clothing that enhances their beauty in the same way as any non-disabled person. Improving clothing functionality and fashion styles will give disabled people a sense of social identity and confidence.

Organizations such as the Runway of Dreams Foundation and Models of Diversity combated the lack of visibility by including disabilities of all types in the 2018 New York Fashion Week. They partnered with adaptive clothing fashion lines from Tommy Hilfiger, Target, and Nike.

Disabled models are rarely seen on billboards, catwalks, or social media. But many women are not allowing it to be a stumbling block, and the media is not set in stone. As a result, many disabled women have beaten the odds in a fashion industry driven by conventional beauty standards.

Jillian Mercado, a woman who used a wheelchair and was diagnosed with spastic muscular dystrophy, is an American fashion model. She and many other confident women strive to reduce stigma and increase media visibility. She has made an appearance in the Nordstrom disabled catalog and many others. Nordstrom has presented disabled models in its ads and catalogs since the 1990s, portraying their unique beauty for the world to see. This expands the social perception of beauty and allows us to understand God's diverse creation of beauty.

Casey Brutus, known as Mama Cax, was a Haitian-American disabled model and speaker. She had every reason to allow life's misfortune to silence her and to feel sorry for herself. At fourteen, she was diagnosed with bone cancer that spread to her lung. While most young teenagers celebrated their sweet sixteen, she underwent an unsuccessful hip replacement to eliminate the affected bone. Still, she ended up getting part of her hip and her entire right leg amputated.

Although this surgery changed her image forever, she decided she would not be excluded from the beauty or fashion world, instead choosing to show up and speak out, demonstrating a different form of beauty and self-love.

Her message was bold and powerful. She became an amputee model featured in magazines like *Essence Magazine, Glamour, Cosmopolitan, Teen Vogue*, and many more. During the Obama presidency, she walked in the White House fashion show. Her advocacy for inclusive fashion design helped open doors for other disabled women. She hit the runway, showing off her prosthetic leg. Until her death in December 2019, she made a huge impact.

10

Love Yourself- Redeem Your God-Given Power

Do you not know that your bodies are temples of the Holy Spirit, who is in you, whom you have received from God? You are not your own.
1 Corinthians 6:19

God created our bodies for His glory. Therefore, trusting and serving the Lord will invite the Holy Spirit to dwell inside us. We must honor God with our bodies by taking care of His temple. Beauty should not be our idol. It is a gift of God, and we should be good stewards of our bodies no matter our perception of them.

Society makes it difficult to accept the variation of beauty. You are judged on the first impression, which has a lasting effect on your hiring processing, dating chances, and society's acceptance. Do not allow anybody to reflect their unrealistic perception of beauty on you. Lift your head to the heavens and let that be your only focus. Do not stoop down for the crumbs others have to offer; you are better than that. God created you in His image. He knew what He was doing.

In the meantime, you should not be a slave to society's standard of beauty. Stop comparing yourself to folks not even in their natural state of beauty.

That is insane!

Consider walking away from social media and stop following other women who do not represent authenticity. We should be praying for them, to be quite honest. Consider turning off reality shows. Do not allow other women who have been working out for years at the gym to intimidate you.

Handle your own business. Remember, comparing ourselves is self-sabotaging and useless. You set your own beauty rules every time you walk out with your head up, announcing to the world that you are your own beauty icon. Celebrate God for blessing you, and look your best while looking like you. Be in control of your perception of beauty, and do not acquaint yourself with others' beauty regulations.

The Temple of God

Loving yourself also includes what you consume. Make healthy eating choices because you only have one body, and God wants us to be good stewards of His precious masterpiece. There are tons of nutritionally balanced foods that contribute to healthy lifestyles. Refrain from harmful substances because the toxic chemicals you allow into your body only grieve the Holy Spirit living inside you while promoting free radicals that lead to unattractive physical consequences.

The science of healthy eating allows us to balance meals that provide fundamental properties for our physical features. For instance, eating vitamin-C-rich foods helps decrease wrinkles and sagging over time. Chia seeds are tiny seeds packed with nutritional benefits such as protein and fiber, suitable for your skin. Adding fruits, vegetables, and leafy greens are all recommended options. Limiting alcohol, sugary foods, and fried food will take some discipline, but it is all worth it in the long run.

In addition to making healthy food choices, drinking water is one of the most effective beauty regimens you can ever practice. Staying hydrated helps you maintain your skin's natural elasticity so that you won't have to pay thousands of dollars later for facial procedures with serious risks. It's good for your nails, hair, and weight management. Water serves as a vehicle; it flushes toxins and carries nutrients to our cells.

I know that this is not a health and wellness book. But as temples of God, taking care of ourselves is how we praise God for the body He gave us; we express gratitude to God when we practice healthy lifestyle regimens. Exercise because it is the right thing to do for your health and well-being. It will boost your stamina and endurance, creating a better and healthier you. Exercising promotes blood circulation, leading to rich blood flow to your scalp, hair follicles, and skin surface. It encourages collagen production, giving you healthier and younger-looking skin.

Sleep is also essential. In a world that is so fast-paced and demanding, rest is the last thing on our minds. However, inadequate sleep affects your appearance and health later. Your body needs the time to rest and repair itself from damages accumulated during the day. You create new cells, giving you a more vibrant and youthful look. Sleeping between seven to nine hours gives your skin a glowing complexion because you release hormones critical to collagen production.

Our body is the shell that houses our spirit. That is why God wants us to care for our bodies, His temple.

Love it!

Appreciate it!

Be grateful for it!

It's the only one you will ever have!

Show Up For Yourself

True beauty is from inside out, not outside in. Decide to say positive things about yourself, and the rest will follow. Allow your natural beauty to evolve into a better version of yourself; do not be apologetic. Stand up for yourself because if you don't, nobody else will.

Practice healthy mental habits that will enhance your well-being by breaking from all outside distractions and being present to nurture your authenticity. Mute the little voice in your head that tells you that you are not good enough or are not worthy of happiness. That is a lie from the devil to keep you mentally enslaved to his deception.

How can you foster happiness in your life? You could start by smiling to the world. When you smile at the world, you give out contagious positive energy, and the world will smile back at you. Just try it! You challenge yourself to feel good by smiling and acting like you are already happy.

Showing up for yourself is a journey. It will often require you to make hard decisions and take on brave moves. You may find yourself standing alone, usually with goosebumps. But you are not alone because God is always with you, even in the darkest moments.

Do not give up! The choice is in your hands.

Accepting and celebrating yourself in a culture that likes to portray images of others living their passionate dreams is challenging. It may appear that we are missing out on the opportunity to live our best life. However, opportunities come to those who are prepared to receive them, and showing up for yourself will attract opportunities to come your way. There is a chance for all of us to experience life's goodness, irrespective of our background, appearance, status, or situation. You are more significant than your case or what others say about you. But you will never know that until you stand up for yourself and see where God takes you.

Imperfectly Perfect

When you look in the mirror, accept that you are imperfectly perfect, just the way you are. You are not broken and in need of fixing. Your identity is more profound than your looks and more eternal than your present situation. You have a divine purpose on Earth, and you can tap into the goodness of God by meditating on His word. We release energy into the atmosphere by our perception and attitude. Therefore, we must be conscious of our attitude toward ourselves.

Do not invest all your self-worth in your outer self. Start investing in your mind and spirit; your true beauty will shine through, allowing your eternal blessings to flow into future generations. Leave that legacy because somebody is going to depend on it for inspiration.

When your confidence is from within, you will not need to boast of compensating for your insecurities. You will know that you are genuinely enough and are deeply loved. You will not participate in beauty comparison but appreciate all beauty for its natural uniqueness.

That realization is freedom.

Things may not be ideal, but do not let that keep you from reaching your dreams.

Enjoy every moment in life.

Self-love is the foundation of who we are. Everything else about us reflects how reliable that foundation is. Although we are talking about the self, it's not about being selfish. Instead, self-love connects you with God and is a blessing to all those around you because when you know how to love yourself, you are better positioned to show love to others. When you combat the destruction of self-sabotaging behaviors, you can enjoy life, which is very attractive. A strong foundation is a great self-esteem booster, allowing us to be our best selves.

When we look at Leah, she was chasing after rhinestones when she kept seeking Jacob's approval, only to face disappointment one after another. It wasn't until she decided to redirect her focus to God that she found her diamond.

Many of you can relate to a time when you gave your all for something you thought would fulfill you. Be that a business, friend, family, lover. Each piece of validation you seek in your life is a rhinestone. You will find your diamond when you redirect your efforts and pursue something of true value.

The media likes to flash money, fame, and idealized beauty, thinking it will bring true happiness. However, this form of happiness usually leaves us empty. True happiness is when you find your true inner beauty.

Beauty diversity glorifies God's creation, testifying to the admirable and incomparable work of art. The body of Christ is made of many members, a symbolic reference to explain that we have diverse talents and gifts, all of whom make up the ministry of God on Earth. Each natural skill and ability serves a purpose in the world and the kingdom of God. You are made in a uniqueness that cannot be duplicated.

Stop chasing after the rhinestones and position yourself to receive God's precious diamond.

Leave a Legacy

A good name is better than fine perfume...
Ecclesiastes 7:1

We were placed on Earth to make contributions. In the beginning, the world was void and without form. God created all the agriculture, animals, land, and water. He created Adam and Eve. Next, He instructed us to have dominion over the earth. Once He made all the resources, He created us to be creative with the raw materials He set before us.

Some people are clear about their purpose in life early on. Some others go through life looking for some eureka moment to reveal their purpose. I advise that if you do not know your goal or talent, do not be discouraged.

Be active. Participate in volunteering activities. Helping others is rewarding and will allow you to exercise your skills and connect with others. Try new things. Get involved in your community and church. Be open to learning and meeting new people. Doing so will teach you more about yourself, what you can tolerate, and what you are good at.

Our abilities and lives are not our own; they belong to God. Take what God has given you and praise him. It does not matter what ugly situations you may have encountered. God wants to do something beautiful in your life. God sent His only begotten son to save us. He came so that we have life more abundantly. But we must trust God enough to surrender ourselves to Him and allow Him to work in and through us.

Do not beat yourself up if you find it hard to trust in the Lord. You may find yourself wrestling with negative thinking. All you need is a little faith—it will go a long way. A mustard seed of faith (Matt. 13:31-32), the tiniest seed, can unleash the omnipotence of God's power in your life and situation, moving mountains and re-positioning trees from the root. Nothing is too big for God, so never underestimate what you have.

Throughout the Bible, God would use what his children already had to do wonders. He asked Moses,

"What is in your hand?"

All Moses had was an ordinary rod that he used to manage the sheep. God called Moses to deliver the Israelites out of Egypt, and Moses denied the role. He didn't see that he qualified for such responsibility. Therefore, he started complaining about everything wrong with him. God cut right to the chase. He instructed him to throw the rod to the ground. Moses threw the rod to the ground, turning it into a snake. He picked it up, and it turned back into a regular rod (Exodus 4:1-3). The rest is history.

God has equipped us in many ways. He has given us talents and buried them inside us because we do not find them good enough to use or worth the risk to invest. We spend too much time focusing on our situation and how others may not like us to realize that God has chosen us to make a difference in the world.

You were not created just to exist. Even if others reject you, focus on God and watch Him change things. Stop worrying about what you do not have or may lack. Obtain an eternal mindset. Do not look at your present situation to determine your destiny or wait until everything in your life is in order before you can live an extraordinary life. He will not ask you to use something you do not already have. So, stop waiting for others to approve of you or for your money to meet the right people, and use your unique passion to activate your influence in the world.

I urge you to leave the race with your peers for materialist affairs. It is all vanity at the end of the day. Physical attractiveness is like a beautiful perfume: appealing and enticing, but temporary. Therefore, I urge you to allow God to open your womb to give birth to a business, creative and wise ideas. He wants to raise your children to great heights. He wants to promote you to leadership roles and shift leadership dynamics. He is getting ready to make you the game-changer.

When you step out of faith and allow God to use you for His divine purpose, you use God's supernatural power to help build something that will take the next generation to a higher level. We are not still in the Stone Age due to legendary figures who stepped out of their comfort zone. Leaving something of substance behind is what makes us honorable and remembered. Build something that will last beyond you.

A legacy is the bond that connects us to the future. It is like passing the baton to those who come after us, interlocking generations with stories, hopes, dreams, innovations, and traditions. Even though our bodies decay over time after we die, the great work and wisdom we share will continue to live on. Look to the Bible, ancient history, and historical figures for proof.

We are responsible for doing everything we can to leave a lasting legacy. This depends not on our possessions or wealth but on our acts of kindness, generosity, and commitment to improving the world. For the next generation to succeed, we must strive to be role models, leaving a legacy of kindness, generosity, and hope for the future.

Spend time with the Lord, and He will reveal greatness through you. He has heard his children's cries and is ready to use you for something amazing. The lead scientist who discovers the cure for cancer can be you. Your frustration with political uproars and passion for human rights can lead you to become a forerunner as a human activist who will save the oppressed.

However, understand that distractions and opposition will come as a stumbling block to discourage you and discredit your abilities. You may stick out when sitting among other leaders, but your confidence in the Lord will give you a seat on the decision-making table despite your background or appearance. The message that God has revealed in you is the word that needs hearing to make a change.

Now that you have embraced your unique beauty and humbled yourself before the Lord, it's time to walk the walk. Leah and Jesus dealt with rejection; we can learn from their examples.

Jesus never allowed rejection to silence him, so you should do the same through your legacy. God wants to write your name in His eternal book of life.

Leah was the less attractive sister. She was rejected and tangled in a scam. There seemed to be no hope for her. However, she did not allow her heart to break beyond repair. She was destined for greatness because God saw her at the most vulnerable point in her life. He opened her womb to give birth to the most significant biblical figures the world had ever met.

You got this!

God is ready to choose a short woman to carry on a giant message, a curly-haired woman to set the record straight, and a physically disabled woman to enable her to do the impossible. Never allow anyone to make you feel like you are not enough. Do not compare yourself to other women or imitate another woman's appearance. God created us all differently and not moved by our outward appearance. There is no one else like you!

We are each unique expression of the one and only infinite God. He made no mistake with your creation. Your purpose in life may not be evident as the sunlight, but it is slowly unfolding through life's experience and your obedience to serving God.

During your metamorphosis, you will get hints as you transform from a caterpillar to a butterfly. Potentials, gifts, and talents start to become apparent. Things begin to change and take on a new part while in your cocoon. Remember, the cocoon is when you endure your transformation; it is a lonely place to be, but the most incredible blessings come during this phase. You will be glad you went through the process when you become the person God created you to be.

I hope you are encouraged and have a new outlook on life. It is natural to want acceptance and love from those around us. But know that sometimes, when God has chosen you for His divine blessing, He will allow you to be rejected by others so that you have nowhere to turn but to turn to Him.

The distractions of this world will cause you to miss God speaking in a still, small voice. He needs your full and undivided attention. That is why, no matter how much you pray to be acceptable to a particular social, professional, or religious affiliation, you never seem to meet the standards set by the group. Instead, you find yourself hitting a dead end every time. It does not matter how determined you are to find acceptance. You may even wonder if God has turned a deaf ear.

Through the story of Leah, you will find that God's plan for Leah was much more significant than she could ever imagine, even in her wildest dreams. This is the same for many of us. You have no idea the ample seed that He has impregnated you with, the rare gemstone that lies in the most sacred place of our womb.

What God puts inside of you is indestructible and precious as gold.

The untold secret of her beauty is our testimony.

Prayer is Important

Prayer is an important facet of self-care and an essential tool for humankind. Our prayer commitment nourishes our souls and allows the Holy Spirit to dwell comfortably and move in ways beyond our imagination. Prayer rejuvenates us and makes us brand new.

However, you do not have to be a professional prayer warrior to pray. You don't have to know all the prayer jargon to go before God. Even if you do not know what to say or how to say it, get on your knees and speak to God.

Leah's prayers, in the beginning, were not focused on God. But God did not judge her. However, as she prayed consistently, we saw a transition. Eventually, the more you pray, the more you exercise your faith in God. God is looking for a humble heart. When you pray, thank God for filling you with His beauty. Please do not waste your time chasing after the attractiveness of the world because they are all vanities. Nonperishable beauty is only found in God.

LEAH'S PRAYER

In a world so focused on physical beauty, my untold secret beauty is found in the most uncommon place. I am beautiful, and I thank you, Father, for giving me a natural radiance.

Flawless in your eyes, constructed in your standards, I rendered my love to your grace.

Thank you for your glorious power that has crafted my glow to capture your essence and illuminate your word in a world where the language of beauty is interpreted within a singular-minded society.

Thank you for enlightening me and rolling back the curtain of self-discovery.

You've shown me that I am a pearl full of luster inside an oyster's shell. That my tendered eyes were traced by your fingers, my lips were softened by your touch, and my cheeks were plumped by your pinch. You made me into a beauty that manifests in various ways.

Like a vibrant field of blossoming flowers at springtime or a song of praise, you laid down rose petals along my path and fragrant my every fickle step that is laced with your name as a constant reminder of your beauty, and I am inducted in your hall of fame.

Sometimes, I can feel the piercing rejection emanating from other's eyes because of my sight. My eyes can see the pity displayed on their face despite their words that encased the lies they speak of my beauty, but they don't believe. And beads of tears stream down my face as I rest away in the grasp of loneliness.

Maybe for a second, I can hear the whispers of loose lips, their laughter lingering in my mind till it lends me towards insanity, till I feel lost and barely can breathe, and suddenly, all I need is to be nothing.

But then again, I am reminded there was no mistake in my creation, and although I see imperfection, you made perfection. Although I feel unsightly, you excite me with your light and express that I do not define my existence by pining for unrefined admiration from others.

You've patiently defined my every being with your love. With the same finger that grazed over the Earth and gave dirt a beating heart, you orchestrated the wind to construct the same lungs, then reduced me beneath the angels so that I could be crowned above. Like a walking sculpture of your blessing and a design of your grace, I was created in your image. You gave me your face!

An image that I can thank God for. My inner beauty is so brilliant that it competes with the sun's shining force—a tug-of-war of fierce beauty radiating from the Son of God's love for humanity.

I was misinterpreted by the blind whose vision cannot accommodate the energy of beauty's electromagnetic wavelength—allowing beauty's blazing roar to speak against deceptive body shaming.

The freedom to be loosened from the chains of society's limited perception of beauty is the freedom to stand in truth.

I was beautifully and wonderfully made.

Amen!

Appendix

APPENDIX A: THE SONS OF LEAH

Ruben

As a young man, Reuben became involved in a rivalry between the two sisters. One day, he came across mandrakes in the field during the wheat harvest. The mandrake was an ancient human-shaped root with an exotic fragrance believed to boost a woman's fertility. Reuben saw the mandrakes and brought them to his mother, who did not have challenges with fertility. God had already blessed her womb, but perhaps the root would make her more attractive to Joseph.

When Rachel found out about Reuben's discovery, she asked Reuben to share what he had gathered. Leah disapproved. Leah confronted her sister, accusing her of taking her husband and now trying to take the mandrake that Reuben found, too.

Since Rachel knew how much it meant for Leah to spend time with Jacob, she struck a deal. She would allow Leah a one-night stand with Jacob for some of the mandrakes. Leah, who was desperate and would do whatever it took to be with Jacob, agreed. After all, one night was better than none.

After Rachel's death, Reuben committed the severe crime of sleeping with his half-sister, Bilhah. She was Rachel's servant, Jacob's concubine, and the mother of two of Jacob's sons. His mother's suffering and fears lead him to commit incest and challenge his father's authority. For that, on Jacob's deathbed, Reuben was denied the birthright due to him as the oldest son (Genesis 49:3).

Although he made many positive moves, Jacob described his character as "unstable as water" (Genesis 49:4), and Jacob did not disinherit him. He only demoted him of his blessings as the first child, allowing him to retain the benefits as a son but not as a firstborn son.

Reuben bore four sons: Hanoch, Pallu, Hezron, and Carmi. The tribe started substantial, always mentioned first in Israel's Twelve Tribes, since he was the firstborn. They collectively took possession of the Promised Land as God had promised. However, the curse of his incestuous involvement with Bilah was never forgotten. The tribe eventually died off over time. Out of the tribe, there was never any mention of judges, prophets, or ruler descendants. They were last mentioned in Revelation 5:5 in the New Testament among the tribes promised the Seal of God for 12,000 of their members.

Simeon

Simeon would grow up to be the second head of the Twelve Tribes of Israel. The Tribe of Simeon remained small, and they had to share their territory in the Promised Land with a larger tribe, Judah (Joshua 19: 1-19). Although small, the Simeonites were as fierce as their father, Simeon.

In the days of Hezekiah, the King of Judea, a band of 500 Simeonites attacked the Hamites and Meunites, destroying them and capturing the Amalekites who tried to escape. After the conquest, they inhabited the land they had conquered (1 Chronicle 4:38-43). God continued to show grace to Simeon's lineage by including the tribe of Simeon in the list of honored Twelve Tribes of Israel whom God will protect during the tribulation (Revelation 7:7).

Levi

There is not much detail on the life of Levi, only mentioning that he was with his other brothers. Levi and his other brothers were also included in the plot against Joseph. Later, he and Simeon attacked the city of Shechem in retaliation for their sister's rape. Jacob was furious with his son's vengeance. On his deathbed, Jacob prophesied that the nation of Levi would scatter, which they did.

Levi's descendants were many (1 Chronicles 6), but just as Jacob prophesied, they would become scattered. They were given no land during the land distribution to the various tribes of Israel. Through the lineage of Levi, you will begin to see how God planned to remove the shame and inferiority that she bore for far too long—by not attaching, uniting, or joining Jacob to Leah.

Judah

Judah was a remarkable son. Although he was the fourth son, he possessed outstanding attributes.

Judah was also involved in the plot against Joseph's life. Like Rueben, he did not want Joseph's blood to be shed on their account. Rueben suggested that they throw Joseph in the pit to come back to remove him from the hole. However, his timing was off. Judah saved the teenager's life by selling him off to the Ishmaelites instead of leaving him in the pit to die.

Judah would later demonstrate additional leadership among his brothers when he convinced Jacob of Joseph's request for Benjamin to be brought to Egypt. He promised his father that Benjamin would return home safely. He pleaded with Joseph when Benjamin was framed to steal the palace's possession, step up, and offer himself as a bondsman.

At one point, Judah departed from his brothers to settle with a Hirah, a man of Adullam. He married a Canaanite woman in his new hometown and had three sons: Er, Onan, and Shelah.

Later, Er would wed Tamar. However, due to his wickedness, God struck Er dead. At his death, he did not leave any offspring behind.

Judah's second son, Onan, was instructed by Judah to replace Er and marry Tamar to bear children in his brother's place. Onan was also wicked. Knowing that the offspring would not be his, he spilled his sperm to the ground whenever he made love to Tamar. It greatly displeased God, so God struck him dead, too.

When both of his eldest sons died, Tamar was not only a widow but childless. Therefore, Judah decided to come up with another plan. Tamar would have to wait till Judah's youngest boy, Shelah, was of age to marry Tamar and finally bear children. Tamar was sent back to her father's house to wait, where she was obedient to her father-in-law's instructions.

Judah's wife died at some point, and Shelah was of age to marry. Judah, who promised that he would give Shelah to marry Tamar, remained silent.

After much patience, Tamar realized Shelah would never be given to her. So, she got clever. She plotted to dress like a harlot and seduced Judah. As collateral for payment, he gave her his rod, signet, and bracelet. When she became pregnant, he unknowingly demanded that she be punished for harlotry until Tamar presented his collateral. Judah took responsibility and publicly admitted his guilt. This saved Tamar and his twin sons from the death penalty. Judah realized that she was more righteous than he was. He married Tamar, and she gave birth to twins Perez and Zerah.

Leah Bore Two More Sons

Then Leah said, "God has presented me with a precious gift. This time my husband will treat me with honor because I have borne him six sons." So she named him Zebulun.
Genesis 30:19

Leah wrestled between trusting in God and craving Jacob's love. But God's love is patient. He did not judge her, and neither is God judging you. After giving birth to Judea, Leah stopped having children for many years to the point that she was considered barren.

What happened during these years after giving birth to Judea? Did Leah start to lose faith?

Leah's situation remained the same. Jacob continued spending most nights with Rachel. After Ruben found the mandrake roots and gave them to Rachel in exchange for Leah spending a night with Jacob, she gave birth to Issachar. Issachar means "man of hire." This was related to the circumstances that took place before his conception.

Issachar became one of the Twelve Tribes of Israel. The tribe was blessed to become men of industrious agriculturists. They were men of labor and lived in the most fertile part of Canaan because of their strong work ethics and wisdom. They were in great numbers when they left Egypt, about 54,400 men, when the census was conducted in Sinai (Numbers 1:29). During the Davidic era, they increased to 87,000 (1 Chronicle 7:5).

In Revelation 7, they were among the tribes who promised God's seal for 12,000 of its members. Issachar was grounded in strong tradition and guided Israel to a righteous path.

After the birth of Issachar, Leah gave birth to her last son, Zebulun. With six sons, Leah knew for sure that she was blessed.

APPENDIX B: LEVITES PRIESTHOOD

Eleazar: High Priest in the Promise Land

On the 40th year after the Israelites came out of Egypt, Aaron was 123 years old. God ordered Moses to take Aaron and Eleazar up to Mount Hor. There, he removed Aaron's garment and put it on Aaron's oldest surviving son and Moses's nephew, Eleazar. This consecrating ceremony would confirm before the people that Eleazar would be Aaron's successor upon his death (Number 33:38; 20:26).

Aaron died on Mount Hor; Eleazar assumed his father's role as High Priest, the Levities leaders' chief, overseeing those who performed the sanctuary duties (Numbers 3:30). He was the first High Priest to rule in the Promised Land when they entered months later.

During the journey through the wilderness, Eleazar was Aaron's chief assistant. His specific duties were to take charge of the oil for the light, fragrant incense, regular grain offerings, and the anointing oil. He oversaw the entire tabernacle and everything in it, including holy furnishing and articles (Number 4:16). He carried out the offering of a red heifer for clearing from uncleanness (Number 19:2-8).

While in office, Eleazar served as a mediator, advisor, and intercessor before the Lord. He assisted in Joshua's inauguration as Moses's successor and helped with the land division when the Israelites finally took possession of the Promised Land (Number 34:17).

Eleazar was a faithful and holy man of God. After his death, Eleazar's son, Phinehas, became the third High Priest (1 Chronicle 9:20). God much blessed him for his zealous role in disciplining a defiant Israelite and ending the plague. God promised to bless his descendants (Number 25: 7-13). All the High Priests would come from Eleazar's descendants except for Eli to Abiathar, who was from the line of Ithamar, Eleazar's brother and Aaron's son. Aaron and all his descendants were the only Levite priesthood allowed to present offerings on the Most Holy Place's altar, making atonement for Israel (1 Chronicles 6:49). Leah's offspring were indeed joined with God.

Eli: Samuel's Mentor

Eli was mentioned in the book of Samuel. He was the High Priest of Shiloh, who would later raise Samuel, Elkanah and Hannah's son, to become his successor in the tabernacle. He was the second to last judge before the rules of kings took leadership. Samuel would later become the final judge of all Israelites.

Although Elkanah lived in Ephraim's territory, he was a Kohathite, an ancestor of Kohath, Levi's son (1 Chronicle 6:22-23). Therefore, Samuel was called to the priesthood due to his bloodline. Even as a young boy, Samuel was favored by God and men (1 Samuel 2:26).

When Hannah dedicated Samuel to the Lord as promised during her barren years, he was brought to the Tabernacle to serve under Eli's leadership (1 Samuel 1:22-25). He was only a child at the time, but he was given his ephod. The ephod was a garment reserved as the high priest's official dress to be worn in the tent meeting at Shiloh, where the Ark of the Covenant was housed (1 Samuel 2:18). It was gold, blue, and purple with scarlet yarns (Exodus 29:5).

Samuel's relationship with God was special because of his devotion. God did not casually reveal prophecies or visions, and it was rare for God to interact with His children directly at that time. Samuel was an exception. Therefore, when God called out to Samuel, he did not recognize God's voice. The Lord called him thrice; Samuel kept assuming Eli was calling him until Eli instructed him that it was the Lord. Samuel then responded to the Lord the next time he heard the call.

The Lord revealed harsh judgment to relay to Eli and the people of God. Samuel did not allow fear or intimidation to influence his assignment. Their relationship grew as God continued to reveal His word to Samuel.

Samuel's credibility also spread among the Israelites because he was a holy messenger of God. He appointed their first king, King Saul, as requested by the people (1 Samuel 10:1). Samuel would later anoint the second king, King David (1 Samuel 16:13). Samuel was joined with God to minister to the people of God, and the sovereignty of God was manifested in Israel.

Samuel resembled his ancestral mother, Leah, because he was a man of prayer. As a Levite, his healthy prayer life granted him a holy relationship with God.

Ezra: From the Return of Captivity

There came the point where the King of Israel was dethroned; the people were captured and exiled by King Nebuchadnezzar of Babylon. Judah had ceased to exist.

After seventy years of captivity, the King of Persia, Cyrus, issued a declaration that allowed the Israelites to return to Jerusalem. The Levites supervised the temple's rebuilding, savaging whatever had been destroyed, and led worship ceremonies to God in Jerusalem (Ezra 3:9-10).

Once the temple was rebuilt, spiritual apathy stepped in. God needed a devoted leader to spark a spiritual revival. He chose Ezra, whose name means "help" in Hebrew. He was a direct descendant of Aaron's priestly family (Ezra 7:1-5), a teacher of the law, and an expert of the Israelites' commands and decrees (Ezra 7:11). He possessed the characteristics of the Levite tribe and the Godly loyalty of his foremother, Leah.

Ezra was an influential man of God who led 2,000 people, including priests, Levites, musicians, gatekeepers, and temple servants, during the second return from captivity (Ezar 7:7). As a Levite, he facilitated the reunion of the Israelites and had a great passion for the mission.

However, to his surprise, he was greatly disappointed when he arrived in Jerusalem. He found that the Israelites had married women who worshiped other gods. He was grieved, urging the people to turn from their sins. He focused on bringing glory and honor to God's name through his teachings and intercessory prayers.

He taught the Law of Moses to the people and was entrusted with appointing civil leaders. Ezra worked alongside Nehemiah, the governor, to build the city walls, and even King Artaxerxes respected his humility. His great work proved significant spiritual progression, and the people renewed their covenant with God. Like his ancestral mother, Leah, he was a devoted child of God who diligently sought Him.

God sanctified the tribe of Levi because of their distinctiveness to protect the truth of God. They had a distinguished covenant with Him that was unique from the other tribes of Israel. The Levites were blessed with the priesthood's rights and assisting in temple duties in the Old Testament. The covenant was continued even into the New Testament.

APPENDIX C: DAVIDIC DYNASTY

Solomon was the son of David and Bathsheba. Upon his father's death, he was anointed king and would succeed David for forty years. Like his father, he was a talented man. He is responsible for the Song of Solomon, the Book of Ecclesiastes, and most chapters in the Book of Proverbs.

God did something not seen with other leaders; he asked King Solomon to ask for whatever he wanted in a dream. Solomon could have asked for anything in the world; instead, he asked God for wisdom to rule His people. This devotion was music to the Lord's ears. He not only granted his wish but also blessed him with substantial wealth (1 Kings 10:27).

After King Solomon's death, David's grandson, Rehoboam, would become king. Due to King Solomon's disobedience in his later years, God divided the kingdom after his death. King Rehoboam would be the first king after the revolution and rule only the tribes of Judahites and Benjamites.

Later, King Abijah, a descendant of David, attempted to reconstruct their former alliance with the tribes. In his famous speech, he reminded them that the kingship was given to the House of David to last forever (2 Chronicles 13:5).

King Jehoshaphat followed the way of his forefather, David. He sought after God and not the foreign gods that infiltrated the Israelites' spiritual lives. Repeatedly, we see that God always appreciates those who seek his ways. He blesses those who diligently seek after Him. God gave King Jehoshaphat rulership over the kingdom. He had great wealth and honor because all of Judah brought gifts to him.

Under his rule, he executed reformation on military, political, and religious aspects. He assigned Levites to travel throughout Judah to teach them the Book of the Law of the Lord (2 Chronicles 17:7-9).

King Hezekiah would later initiate another reformation to clean up the mess his father, King Ahaz, left behind. His righteousness was a gateway to a close relationship with God (2 Chronicles 31:20). During his rule, prophets such as Isaiah and Micah ministered to the people of Judah. He destroyed pagan artifacts and idols. He reopened and cleaned out the temple. Levitical priesthood temple service and the Passover national holiday observance were reinstituted (2 Chronicles 30:1). He experienced great success during his rulership because the Lord was with him and brought revival to Judah.

Josiah was the world's youngest to become king—he was only eight years old when he took the throne. The country was in bad condition and in need of another reformation. He was godly; hence, he restored the temple once he came of age. The high priest found the Book of the Law and read it to Judah's people by Josiah. The word of God, which was once neglected due to pagan worshipping, was reintroduced to the people, and God renewed their covenant. Josiah's legacy demonstrates that God does not discriminate with age. He could use anyone, even as young as eight, if fully committed and obedient to God.

There were many kings from the lineage of David not mentioned in this book. Although some kings were evil, many kings pleased God. God kept his promise to David until the Messiah established his rulership on Earth. Through her hardship, Leah's faith in God made her a glorious mother of royal kingship. Everyone who humbled themselves before the Lord, He blessed magnificently.

The Birth of Jesus

King David generally and passionately loved God. It was an unconditional covenant because no other king, even King Solomon, could ever live up to the standards of David. For that, God's promise did not depend on Judah or Israel's obedience.

Before the birth of Jesus, this historical and divine season, God's messenger made several appearances. The angel Gabriel visited Joseph, who did not believe Mary in her pregnancy, as it was biologically impossible. How can a young woman become pregnant unless she has been with another man? However, when the angel visited Joseph to confirm that she was pregnant with the Messiah, Joseph accepted the news. Joseph was also from the House of David, a direct descendant of David's son, Solomon. Joseph's encounter with the angel allowed Joseph to accept the pregnancy and support Mary. After all, Isaiah prophesied that the Messiah in the Old Testament would be an unusual birth.

The angel told Mary of Elizabeth's pregnancy. Mary rushed to see Elizabeth in the hill country of Judea. When she got there, John the Baptist leaped into Elizabeth's womb upon Mary's greeting, and Elizabeth was filled with the Holy Spirit. It was a match made from heaven and confirmed the angel's prophecy. It was a preview of the divine interaction that would later occur at the water baptism when the Son of David asked John the Baptist to baptize Him in the Jordan River.

Jesus's birth could not have started with a humbler beginning than this. When Mary gave birth to Jesus, a brilliant star appeared over his birthplace, signifying his heavenly kingship. The angel appeared to three shepherd men, known as the three wise men. He told them about the Messiah's birth and how to find him. The men took off on their quest, ignoring King Herod's request to share Jesus's birthplace. They found Jesus exactly where the star had pointed.

When they saw the baby resting on the manger, they knelt and worshipped him. They brought three gifts: gold, frankincense, and myrrh. Each gift was highly valued by royal kings and emperors and signified his birth, ministry, and burial.

Jesus would be the last heir to the throne of David. Though he was born a king, he was not born under ideal conditions. He was birthed among animals—a most unusual situation, though this was part of his assignment.

However, the three wise men did not judge his birthplace. They were shepherds, so the environment wasn't new to them. When they saw baby Jesus, they obediently knelt and worshipped him despite the animal odor and stable condition. Although Joseph and Mary knew that baby Jesus was the Messiah, they did not wait until they could find a more sanitary location before receiving visitors.

References

American Society of Plastic Surgeons. (2014, February 26). Plastic Surgery Procedures Continue Steady Growth in U.S. Retrieved from https://www.plasticsurgery.org/news/press-releases/plastic-surgery-procedures-continue-steady-growth-in-us.

Dakanalis, A., & Riva, G. (2013). Mass media, body image, and eating disturbances: The underlying mechanism through the lens of the objectification theory. In *Handbook on Body Image: Gender Differences, Sociocultural Influences, and Health Implications* (pp. 217-235). Nova Science Publishers, Inc.

Eisenberger, N.I & Lieberman, M.D. (July 2004). Why rejection hurts: a common neural alarm system for physical and social pain. *TRENDS in Cognitive Sciences, 8*(7), 294-300. doi:10.1016/j.tics.2004.05.010

Khalid, A., and Quinonez, C. (2015). Straight, white teeth as a social prerogative. *Sociology of Health & Illness. 37*(5). 782-796. Doi: 10.1111/1467-9566.12238.

LaRose, J. (2016). U.S. Weight Loss Market Worth $66 Billion Commercial Chains Rebound, But Number of Dieters Shrinks. Marketdata Enterprises, Inc. *The Informatics Specialist.* Retrieved from https://www.marketdataenterprises.com/wp-content/uploads/2018/03/Diet-Mkt-2017-Press-Release.pdf

Macdonald, G., & Leary, M. R. (2005). Why Does Social Exclusion Hurt? The Relationship Between Social and Physical Pain. *Psychological Bulletin, 131*(2), 202–223. DOI: 10.1037/0033-2909.131.2.202.

Medical bag site. (2013, August 19). Neck Elongating Still Practiced Within This Indigenous Tribe. Retrieve from https://www.medicalbag.com/home/features/body-modification/neck-elongating-still-practiced-within-this-indigenous-tribe/

Park, S. (2014). Flapper Fashion in the Context of Cultural Changes of America in the 1920s. *City University of New York (CUNY) Academic Works*. Retrieved from: https://academicworks.cuny.edu/gc_etds/263

Perrin, A. & Anderson, M. (2019). The share of U.S. adults using social media, including Facebook, is mostly unchanged since 2018. PEW Research Center. Retrieved from: https://www.pewresearch.org/fact-tank/2019/04/10/share-of-u-s-adults-using-social-media-including-facebook-is-mostly-unchanged-since-2018/

Pipia, A. (2015). The Push for Plus: How a Small Part of the Fashion Industry Hopes to Make Big Changes to the Plus-Size Women's Fashion Market. *CUNY Academic Works*. Retrieved from: https://academicworks.cuny.edu/gj_etds/8

Rothblum, E. D. (2018). Slim chance for permanent weight loss. *Archives of Scientific Psychology, 6*(1), 63-69. http://dx.doi.org/10.1037/arc0000043

Talamas, S.N, Mavor, K.I, Perrett, D.I. (2016). Blinded by Beauty: Attractiveness Bias and Accurate Perceptions of Academic Performance. *PLoS ONE. 11*(2). Doi: 10.1371/journal.pone.0148284.

Wagner, C., Aguirre, E., & Sumner, E. (2016). The relationship between Instagram selfies and body image in young adult women. *First Monday, 21*(9). doi:10.5210/FM.v21i9.6390.

Untold Secret Beauty Publisher

ABOUT THE PUBLISHER

We are the champions of women, empowering them to turn rejection into acceptance and embrace their triumphant journeys, even if they seem sad to others. Our mission is to inspire women to share their stories and showcase themselves as victorious individuals who transform their lives.

Our goal is to amplify the voices of women who have gone from darkness to light. We understand the challenges they face and the societal judgments they endure. As trendsetters, we encourage women to discover their own distinctive beauty, breaking free from society's conventional standards.

Visit our website: www.Untoldsecretbeauty.com/publisher

Our Mission

In Untold Secret Beauty, our mission is to help underrepresented yet talented women discover their hidden beauty amidst rejection and setbacks. We emphasize the art of writing as a means of embracing and expressing women's individual definitions of beauty.

Our Vision

"To Transform the Mindset of Women in Understanding the New Perception of Themselves."

To empower and support a generation of women who will break free from cultural and social barriers. To equip every woman with the tools and the confidence to take charge of her own narrative.

CORE VALUES

Dedication

We believe in setting opportunities for women to reveal and share their untold secret beauty.

Diversity and Inclusion

We celebrate our differences and learn from one another. We believe that more representation of diverse beauty, no matter the ethnic background, complexion, height, weight, age, or hair texture, the greater impact we will have to positively transform the beauty perception in the world.

Self-Love

When you love yourself, you create peace for yourself. You enable the positive light within you to shine bright.

www.ingramcontent.com/pod-product-compliance
Lightning Source LLC
Chambersburg PA
CBHW070939080526
44589CB00013B/1566